Grit, Grace & Gravitas

The Three Keys to Transforming Leadership, Presence, and Impact

JANE FIRTH, MSOD, AND ANDREA ZINTZ, Ph.D.

Open Door Publications

Grit, Grace & Gravitas
The Three Keys to Transforming Leadership, Presence, and Impact

Copyright © 2020 by
Jane Firth, MSOD, and Andrea Zintz, Ph.D.

ISBN: 978-1-7328202-1-0

All rights reserved
Printed in the United States of America

All of the persons used as examples in this book are composites of clients the authors have worked with. The names and identifying characteristics have been changed.

No part of this book may be used or reproduced in any manner whatsoever without the written permission of the author, except in the case of brief quotations embodied in critical articles and reviews.

Published by
Open Door Publications
2113 Stackhouse Dr.
Yardley, PA 19067
www.OpenDoorPublications.com

Cover design: Caroline Chen

More praise for Grit, Grace & Gravitas...

Winning isn't everything if one breaks the organization in the attempt. Various forms of leadership have been embraced and discarded over time. In *Grit, Grace, & Gravitas,* Jane Firth and Andrea Zintz have found the answers to the leadership way forward. They have discovered the essential elements that allow leaders to lead and win without doing damage to themselves or to the organization they serve. Leaders need a balanced integration of *Grit, Grace, & Gravitas* to successfully overcome challenges both inside and outside of their organizations—including their own Board of Directors. This book is an insightful and worthwhile read now but soon will become a cornerstone leadership reference.

Colonel Kenneth L. Brier
USA, Ret and President of Montbatten Holdings LLC

The timing of this book is critical. Many people believe we have new leadership needs, and this book defines what authentic leadership is. What makes this book different is its focus on actionable details. The authors' on-point observations provide practical and tactical advice from leaders. No matter your challenge or opportunity, something in this book can help as you forge your path to have the most significant impact as you lead, and in your own life.

Patricia Q. Connolly Executive Director
Raj & Kamla Gupta Governance Institute, Drexel University

Grit, Grace & Gravitas is a game changer for all leaders. Immensely readable and practical, coauthors Firth and Zintz weave the sciences of sociology, psychology and neuroscience into a strong silk that any leader can utilize on a daily basis. Using real life examples, the authors deconstruct issues and build solutions in straightforward language, incorporating an evidence-based framework. Reinforcing the principles of reaction management, relationship intelligence and the constructive power of grace, leaders are given tools and life lessons that can be readily applied to the workplace and beyond. Transcending different fields and types of organizations, *Grit, Grace & Gravitas* helps the leader develop, nurture and maintain positive relationships with themselves, co-workers, and the world around them—a key to success. This book needs to be considered a primary resource for any type of leadership program at the national and international levels.

Lynn G. Dressler, Dr.P.H.
Founder and Former Director, Mission Health Personalized Medicine Program; Alumnus, University of North Carolina Public Health Leadership Doctoral Program

Grit, Grace & Gravitas beautifully and accurately outlines how "Grace" is the missing ingredient for effective leadership… teaching the reader how to develop it through many real-life examples. If you are looking to take your organization to a new level where your team is working together in a positive, more effective direction, with a unity of purpose, this is a must read.

Mark Fishman
Former CEO Fishman and Tobin
Founder and CEO of TRF LLC, Investment Company

Whether you are an aspiring leader or deep in the trenches of leadership, the authors give you the practical strategies for handling challenges, moving forward in difficult times, empowering others, and generating an environment that breaks through ineffective patterns to innovate, adapt, and thrive.

Helene Lerner
Founder, Womenworking.com and TV host

In *Grit, Grace, & Gravitas*, a secret of effective leadership has been uncovered. What's new in this book is the recognition that it is grace (reaction management and relationship intelligence) that allows for the constructive use of grit and gravitas to lead oneself and others to greatness - while keeping everyone upbeat and engaged along the way. The authors' "BETA" Model of the social needs of groups is a must-have for anyone who leads a team. My favorite part of the book is Chapter 6 where the authors map well-known leadership derailers to having too much or too little grit/gravitas and show how the leader can use grace to bring themselves back into balance. A worthwhile addition to the canon of leadership development literature.

Charles Jones
Author, Emotional Intelligence for Stress-Free Leadership
Chief Scientist, The Institute for Adaptive Mastery LLC

Whether you are at the beginning or approaching the end of your leadership journey, *Grit, Grace, & Gravitas* is an insightful tool to help you navigate your style and the culture of your work environment. I found myself re-focusing on things I have learned over the years and things that I could have done better as a leader.

Rosalyn McPherson
President & CEO, The ROZ Group, Inc.

Based on years of experience as coaches and advisors to business leaders, authors Jane Firth and Andrea Zintz share how the right balance of *Grit, Grace & Gravitas* leads to high-performing teams and organizational success. This book should be read by every leader whose goal is to build stronger, more productive working relationships.

Stan Silverman
Author Be Different! The Key to Business and Career Success
Founder, Silverman Leadership

Grit, Grace & Gravitas contains focused tools for any leader to excel. The BETA approach is critical to finding the best ways to engage your team. I love how *Grit, Grace, & Gravitas* fine tunes and perfects your approach as a leader. The book includes excellent diagnostics to improve your leadership ability. It is clear that with grit and gravitas, when grace is lacking, a leader is less effective and the environment suffers. This book is instructive on how to recognize your blind spots and rebalance your leadership efforts. This approach is an asset to any leader at any stage of his or her career.

Megan Mitchell, Principal, Mitchell Consulting
Program Director, Centre of Excellence for Innovation Leadership, Schulich Executive Education Centre, York University
Co-author Orchestrating Sustainable Innovation: A Symphony in Sound Bites

Grit, Grace & Gravitas is a truly great book, one that I literally could not put down. The balance of the models, research, and stories, along with engaging the reader in their own journey was fantastic.

Bob Schatz, DMgt.
Owner, Agile Infusion LLC

The need for transformational leadership has never been more important, not just for business, but for communities and our country. *Grit, Grace & Gravitas* should be a must-read for all leaders no matter where they are in the arc of their professional and personal journey. Firth and Zintz bring decades of experience in working with leaders to inform and define a pathway to leadership growth that could change the C-suite forever.

Patricia D. Wellenbach
President and CEO, Please Touch Museum

To my husband, Vincent, my sister-in-law Sara, my family here and abroad, and my extended family of close friends, clients, and colleagues: With my love, respect, and gratitude, I dedicate this book to you. Every day I am inspired by your brilliance, your generosity, and your courage. To Andrea, with my love and appreciation for your partnership, for embracing the ideas of grit, grace and gravitas, and for bringing it all to life together. To Caroline Chen and Karen Miller, with gratitude for your steadfast support of our work.

Jane Firth

To my husband, Dave Bernstein, and our daughters, Ali and Jessie, whose wisdom, love, and support have inspired me in all my pursuits. Also, to the incredible leaders who've been my clients from whom I've learned so much and have provided me with a depth of perspective regarding grit, gravitas, and the constructive power of grace. And Jane Firth, my partner in the creation of our framework and who is the personification of grace.

Andrea Zintz

"What you leave behind is not what is engraved in stone monuments, but what is woven into the lives of others."

Pericles

Table of Contents

Preface..1

Chapter 1
An Introduction to *Grit, Grace* and *Gravitas*......7
The constructive power of grace, The integrated relationship between grit, grace and gravitas, When grit or gravitas is out of balance

Chapter 2
Defining Executive Presence......................21
Presence is a leader's individual mark or imprimatur, Your presence is as unique as your fingerprints, Our research on presence, Common myths of executive presence, Personal investment in shaping executive presence, The two essential pillars of grace

Chapter 3
Reaction Management:
The first pillar of *grace*..............................43
An inheritance we all share, Managing reactions, Reaction management & self-awareness, Choosing to step out of the reactive zone, Stepping out of the reactive zone, Flight, Fight, Some reactions are harder to transcend

Chapter 4
The Second Pillar of *Grace*:
Relationship Intelligence.........................73
Robert's wake-up call, What kind of leader/person is it important for me to be? Why does this matter? Stan's desire to be an exemplary leader, Anna takes stock, Review, Keeping your internal bearings present

Chapter 5
Relationship Intelligence:
Leadership & the Social Brain..........................93
What does the social brain tell us about needs? The social brain and psychological safety, How to use the BETA Model to diagnose, Vulnerability and trust, Using the BETA Model to develop high performance, Using the BETA Model to elevate emotional states when you notice a lack of engagement, How NOT to elevate emotional states of mind and stay stuck in the reactive zone, Summary

Chapter 6
The impact
of leadership on culture............................123
Using and leveraging the power of grit, grace and gravitas, Leadership: A choice to be made and its impact in shaping a culture, Imbalances in grit and gravitas are more common in the absence of BETA conditions

Chapter 7
Changing a culture with
the constructive power of *grace*..................145
A surprising turn of events, OK, Now What

Chapter 8
Grace and Generosity..................... 161
When a leader lacks generosity, When generosity is present in a leader, The power of generosity in the midst of crisis, Grace has many faces but the feeling is unmistakable, Healing the divide, Generosity and the constructive power of grace

Chapter 9
Using *Grit, Grace* and *Gravitas*
to Prevail in Adversity..................................187
How Irene's situation became intolerable, How Irene successfully organized her efforts to deal with her situation

Chapter 10
Conclusion:
Grace is the game changer........................199

Addendum..205
Finding Your Internal Bearings Exercise, Reaction management, Relationship intelligence

Resources..231

Preface

We are living and working in unprecedented times—times in which exemplary leadership is needed more than ever. We are encountering unexpected economic challenges, global disruptions, cultural and political divides, and a rapid rate of technological advancements that are impacting our work environments and having an emotional impact on the lives of people we lead. At this moment, as we complete our final edits, the world is going through the hardships and tragedies of a global pandemic. Resources are stretched as we try to meet the challenges of dealing with the coronavirus (COVID-19). We have a world to put right, and we have a chance to rebuild on better terms with each other.

What does all of this mean about leadership? And what does all of this mean about you as a leader? With thousands of eyes watching, you take the reins your role requires of you. Whether your focus is operations, finance, sales and marketing, communications, technology, research, mergers and acquisitions, or human resources, the responsibilities on your shoulders are formidable. Although job descriptions spell out role responsibilities, leaders face responsibilities that are not found there. They have to do with the complexities of human lives—many of which will keep you up at night—that require leadership skills on your part that can mean the difference between succeeding and failing. What empowers you to energize and inspire the men and women you lead to produce the results and outcomes that will matter?

In our extensive work with clients over the years, we've had the privilege of listening deeply to what is in the hearts and minds of the men and women we coach and advise. Our work with leaders in their various industries and work environments, along with our research, led us to identify critical, non-negotiable qualities and behaviors that form the foundation and character of truly exemplary leaders. We've found that while every leader is unique, exemplary leaders possess and lead through a combination of three critical, non-negotiable factors we will be defining and illustrating in depth in the pages that follow. The character and heart of their leadership are composed of the following: 1) they have *grit*—an uncompromising commitment to performance excellence and strategic focus, and 2) they have *gravitas*—a depth of professional knowledge and competence that contributes to excellence in performance, and most importantly, 3) they have *grace*—they relate to others constructively in considerate, empathetic, and genuinely caring ways.

When a leader integrates the skills and qualities of *grace* into their approaches, behaviors, connection with people, and demeanor, they can transform the imbalances in their *grit* and *gravitas* that were getting in the way and causing problems. For example, there can be imbalances such as when a leader comes across as domineering, arrogant, and condescending, or when a leader's brusque impatience or intolerance has people walking on eggshells, or when a leader's hesitancy and indecisiveness leaves people without clear guidance and direction. Every chapter of our book provides insight on how leaders have used the constructive power of grace to deal with challenges. Our framework, the examples throughout each chapter, and the exercise you can use at the end of the book will enable you to elevate and evolve the quality and substance of your leadership, your presence, and your impact.

Here is our promise. After reading this book and applying the knowledge it provides:

• You will have a more compelling and impactful presence—your presence will evolve and be a contribution in ways it has never been before.

• You will be a more effective leader—you will have the keys to bringing out the best in yourself and those you lead.

• You will understand how to be effective—and even masterful—in dealing with the emotional realities and challenges of leadership that otherwise get in the way of solutions, innovation, and progress.

May the constructive power of grace be with you. May it grace your life and the lives of those you lead.

A Final Note

As we concluded writing this book, the onset of the COVID-19 pandemic and its implications for society in general and for business and business leaders in particular became a reality. As in other parts of our world, in the United States we found ourselves sheltering in place, practicing social distancing, working from home, and looking to leaders for guidance and wisdom as everything changed around us.

The tenets of *Grit Grace & Gravitas* provide clarity as we naturally assess leaders as to whether they provide us with insight and resolve or leave us feeling anxious and dismayed. Business leaders are faced with the challenge of making many decisions they would rather not have to make. There is a sensitive equation in finding a balance between fiscal responsibility and remaining present to the potential negative impact on the lives of all employees.

In addition to the complex challenges and consequences of the coronavirus, we are all confronted with the horrifying shock wave of racial injustice. The appalling, brutal murders of black men and women call us to confront and take action against the realities of racial injustice. We stand together at a defining moment that will have an impact on generations to come. We are called to take responsibility for what got us here and build a more equitable and just society.

With all the technological advances we human beings have created, what is the equivalent evolution in our human consciousness and character? How can we face, mend, and heal deeply rooted racial inequities and social injustices in ways that transform us? How can we consciously and intentionally work together in good faith? As leaders we can bring people together, ask the right questions, facilitate the hard conversations that need to take place, channel feedback into change, and implement new and equitable policies in our organizations, schools, and communities. The key to our evolution lies in using our collective, constructive power. May we work constructively together. May we be proud of how we answered the call.

We hope this book provides you with fresh perspectives for leading in times of crisis and provides you with new filters to strengthen your ability to lead and assess the qualities of others. What do the men and women you lead need from you at this critical, uncertain time? What are you communicating through your approaches, your behaviors, the quality of your connection with them? What is your demeanor demonstrating, and how are you affecting those around you?

Provide Hope: Whether we are aware of it in the moment or not, we have the choice to recognize our discomfort with what is out of our control and focus on the things that are within our control. We each have the strength and the resilience to envision new pathways as we navigate today's realities—to understand what is needed, to realize what matters most, and to connect with our abilities to innovate and rebuild.

Provide Calm Reassurance: Being calm and having a calming and reassuring presence are a choice and do not require knowing all the answers. But it does require your integrity, your courage, and your honesty. In these uncertain times, remember that your leadership can serve as a lifeline. You can provide calm reassurance, guidance, and inspiration that empowers those you lead to focus, innovate, and find the best ways forward.

Provide Human Connection: Bring your caring, empathy, and compassion to those with whom you live and work. Be trustworthy. Be there for people. Make people's lives better today and every day. Trust that you can evolve to meet these challenges, connect with the best that is within you, and inspire the best that is within the men and women you lead.

As you guide yourself and others through this pandemic, no matter how daunting things may seem along the way, innovative solutions are there for us to discover. To paraphrase the poet Rumi: Somewhere out beyond the chaos and uncertainty, there is a field of resilience and resourcefulness. We will meet you there.

June 17, 2020

Chapter 1
An Introduction to *Grit*, *Grace* and *Gravitas*

In this chapter, we'll provide an introduction to our model and theory of grit, grace and gravitas, and begin to explore their relationship to leadership and executive presence, beginning with the questions: What are grit, grace and gravitas? Why is it important to consider them together? How does grace increase the value of a leader's grit and gravitas? How does grace elevate a leader's grit and gravitas through its constructive power?

This chapter begins to address these questions, explained in great depth throughout the book. We'll include an example of a leader who utilized feedback in a constructive way and came to understand how he could evolve as a leader and elevate the quality of his impact.

What are *grit*, *grace* and *gravitas*? Why is it important to consider them together? With *grace* as the game changer, they are the three keys to transforming your leadership, your presence, and your impact.

What makes a good leader? What makes an exemplary leader? What does presence have to do with leadership? What if executive or leadership presence isn't the mystery it has been made out to be? There is no shortage of information or opinions when it comes to increasing one's executive presence. But get ready. You are going to learn how *grace,* and the way it enhances the impact of your *grit* and your *gravitas,* is the game-changing strength of exemplary leadership and *executive presence.*

What is your most impressive example of someone you perceive as having a strong executive presence? What qualities did that person possess?

There are noticeable qualities that distinguish exemplary leaders, something that sets them apart. What we've discovered in our years of working with leaders is that exemplary leaders have a distinct combination of qualities and skills—an effective integration of their *grit, grace* and *gravitas.* As the definitions of *grit, grace* and *gravitas* are clarified in depth in the chapters to follow, you will come to understand what they mean for you in the context of your leadership and your current challenges.

The constructive power of *grace*

We have seen time and again that what distinguishes the really great leaders is their capacity for *grace*. The world, your organization, and the men and women you lead need *grace*. And it is scarce. There is one road you can take that leads to *grace*, and we will show you how that road lies within you. Taking that road leads you to know yourself better than you do today. It leads you to a greater depth of understanding of others and fortifies your connection to what matters most to you as a leader.

> Leaders, by virtue of the role they have accepted, have a responsibility for the impact they have on the men and women they lead. The constructive power of *grace* changes the impact of a leader's *grit* and changes the impact of their *gravitas*.

The skills and qualities of *grace* increase a leader's ability to disrupt the negative behavioral patterns and habits that detract from the transforming influence their presence could have. For instance, when a leader's *grit* or *gravitas* is out of balance, their *grit* can come across as overbearing, and their *gravitas* can come across as arrogant. This causes many different kinds of negative reactions in the people they are impacting. Reactions such as anger, resentment, and frustration have a distracting impact on productivity, teamwork, and performance.

When a leader infuses the *constructive power of grace* into their *grit* and *gravitas,* something extraordinary becomes possible. He or she gets out of their own way. They improve the quality of their impact on the men and women they lead and are able to unify those who are stuck in contentious viewpoints. They inspire others to come together around a vision that has resonance and meaning. With *grace* infused into their *grit* and *gravitas,* their impact becomes far more valuable.

Whether you are a seasoned professional who wants to evolve to your next level or just starting out in your leadership role, you will come to recognize the advantages that leaders gain through integrating the skills and qualities of *grace* into their *grit* and *gravitas.* It will become increasingly evident to you how these distinctive skills and qualities of *grace* cause a leader's presence to evolve.

Along with demystifying the myths and confusions regarding executive presence, leadership, charisma, and other qualities, you will come to understand that it doesn't matter if you are, for example, an introvert an extrovert, or a "born leader." Your presence can be compelling, calming, empowering, and stabilizing, adding value day after day as you guide those you lead to achieve the results that matter. You will accomplish this and so much more as you practice and achieve the skillful integration of your own g*rit*, *grace* and g*ravitas*.

Let's begin by looking at the relationship between them.

The integrated relationship between *grit*, *grace* and *gravitas*

Grit, grace and *gravitas* have an unusual, profound relationship. *Grit* and *gravitas*, as you will see, foster essential leadership qualities and skills. But a leader's unmodulated *grit* can be experienced by others as too harsh, rigid, inflexible, and closed-minded. Lacking in *grace*, others may interpret this leader's unmodulated *grit* as offensive, inconsiderate, overbearing, or unappreciative. As a consequence, people can be left feeling resentful, less motivated, and less engaged. Lacking in *grace*, a leader's unmodulated *gravitas* can be perceived as arrogant, overconfident, condescending, intolerant, disinterested, and disrespectful. *Grace* is the defining difference—the game changer—as it modulates a leader's *grit* and *gravitas* through its *constructive power*.

What are some examples? Let's consider how too much *grit* might result in either micromanaging or bullying, or how too little *grit* might result in some form of avoidance or the need to please. The *constructive power of grace* will modulate a leader's *grit* so that team members no longer react negatively. With too much *grit*, team members may receive your message as "it's my way or the highway." With too little *grit*, they may think that their leader is avoiding the critical matters that need his or her attention. An excellent way to understand imbalances is through a process of gathering feedback.

When *grit* or *gravitas* is out of balance

The quality and impact of your presence is determined by how you express your *grit* and *gravitas*. If there is an imbalance, it is easy to correct it with the *constructive power of grace*. If you want to understand your presence and the kind of impact you are having on the people you lead, you can gather feedback to learn how others perceive your approaches, behaviors, the quality of your connection with them, and your demeanor. This information will be useful because it will reveal blind spots, ineffective habits, foibles, and flaws that you may not realize are getting in the way of your aspirations as a leader. Many people have used a version of the phrase "the truth will set you free, but first it will make you mad!" Even though you may not like hearing feedback, once you get past any adverse reactions to it you will have the freedom to evolve—to use what you have learned for your growth and development.

> Getting a handle on blind spots means revising or replacing habits that can derail you, that get in your way of being and doing your best and, as a leader, get in the way of others being and doing their best.

It is in your power to assess, understand, and use the essence of feedback to improve the impact you are having. Feedback reflects how someone is seeing and interpreting "the data" of the effect you have as a result of your way of being and interacting—positive or negative. It is important to remember that feedback contains interpretations. What does this mean? As an example, you will find definitions in step two of our addendum, *Finding Your Internal Bearings Exercise,* so you will see that with an imbalance of too much *gravitas*, a leader can come across as being unapproachable and intimidating. When receiving feedback, however, it is interpreted by the giver;

some of it may not ring true for you or even be true about you. While it may not be true, it's useful to consider that something in your way of being or interacting is being perceived and interpreted in this way.

For example, let's consider a leader who is misinterpreted as unapproachable and intimidating when actually, he or she is comfortable one on one, but ill at ease when talking in groups. Receiving this feedback, he or she can look to their leadership aspirations and choose to consider how to address the interpretation or reputation of aloofness. What are some simple steps toward changing this? For example, establish the habit of warmly greeting people when first entering a room, smiling more, and conveying sincere interest by saying something like "it's nice to see you." What at first feels awkward can become second nature. The reward itself is in the power to transform the impact your presence is having on those you lead and serve.

In considering feedback, it's essential to understand the differences between giving feedback to empower someone to develop and evolve as distinct from confirming a bias. With *confirmation bias,* evidence is gathered to support your beliefs and theories about someone. It involves favoring selective information that confirms your previously existing beliefs or biases, and it contributes to overconfidence in these beliefs. It can maintain or strengthen them, although there is evidence to the contrary. For example, a leader receives feedback and, in good faith, works to improve him or herself, but no matter what they do, their efforts are neither considered, recognized, or validated.

Feedback meant to empower someone is different; it is based on wanting the best outcomes for someone and allowing this person to develop and evolve. It's given in the spirit of support; empowering them to become more aware so that he or she can have the opportunity to grow as a person and as a leader. And also so that they can have the freedom to improve their approaches, behaviors, the quality of how they connect with people, and their demeanor. When someone is supported in this way, their presence will evolve. Feedback opens the door. Getting past your discomfort with feedback lets you walk through it. Let's look at a leader who found a way to gather the feedback he needed to support his development.

Craig was an assistant commissioner. Everyone he worked with thought he was brilliant and valued his knowledge and experience. The problem was he used his brilliance in ways that closed everyone else out. He wanted to be *the guy with the ideas and solutions*. He saw this as his way of creating value and being of service to others.

In our work together, he described his aspiration as a desire to help. But without realizing it, his aspiration was being fed by an imbalance in his *gravitas*. He always felt he was the one with the "right" answers. He backed up his ideas with a great deal of evidence and dominated the room by talking, not listening to others or asking for their input. He would wait impatiently for the other person to finish what they had to say while constructing his justifications and arguments so he could gain approval for his idea. This habitual behavior created frustration for his stakeholders, even when Craig's suggestions were good ones.

His overbearing presence, in spite of his intention to contribute, came across as arrogant and insufferable. Whenever his constituents adopted his ideas, advice, and recommendations, he experienced a high level of satisfaction. While this felt like a reward to Craig, it hurt the quality of his connection with his stakeholders. This particular imbalance in Craig's *gravitas*—thinking one's opinion is the only one that matters, going on and on and seeming pedantic, speaking only on "send" and not listening to "receive"—was getting in his way. His tendency to dominate with his ideas exhibited a pattern of selective listening—taking in only what he was interested in hearing—and leaving others feeling frustrated, disregarded, and resentful.

Craig also had an imbalance in his *grit*—he would lose his focus on his commitments to others, become distracted, and fail to follow through on promises he had made. His tendency to be easily distracted obscured the importance of keeping the long term in perspective. He gained a reputation for struggling with priorities and being unreliable.

Craig's boss, the senior commissioner of the department, called him into his office, and a tough conversation ensued. He told Craig that his habit of not following through, along with his lack of transparency regarding his decisions, was a problem. He also said his poor listening skills, as well as his tendency to dominate and not allow others to contribute their perspectives, would derail his future in the organization. His boss suggested that he work with an executive coach. Although it was difficult for Craig to hear how and why he was getting in his own way, he managed his reactions and took his boss up on the offer of coaching.

Taking stock, Craig grappled with his self-perception of being generous, and how it could be so off-base. He began to notice that his urge to be *the guy with the ideas* was driven by a need to be needed. He told his coach, "I think my drive to contribute to others is blocking their contributions. I'm sucking up all the air in the room. I haven't been a good thought partner. I've seen others as 'obstacles,' and I've been very judgmental."

Craig also admitted to himself that he allowed what was urgent to distract him from what others were counting on him for. This imbalance in his *grit* had him drop commitments he had made to others and caused frustration and annoyance as a result of his not following through as promised. Urgencies drew him like a magnet. In considering how he could, on the one hand, regain his focus and, on the other hand, break his habit of dominating discussions, he worked with his coach on developing some new habits.

Craig decided that he could start asking questions that would open the door to others' participation and would be an excellent way to convey that he wanted to hear their ideas. To do this, Craig prepared some nonjudgmental questions to ask at his next team meeting.

At the start of the meeting, Craig took a few moments to let his team know that he was aware that he had a habit of dominating their meetings. He asked them to bear with him as he tried a different approach. The quality of the discussions was fascinating to him. The answers to the questions he asked expanded the thinking of the group, which contributed improvements to Craig's ideas and solutions. He engaged the others on the team, listening attentively to understand their perspectives instead of justifying his point of view. Craig felt exhilarated by the results of the meeting. A few team members approached him to let him know that this was the best meeting he ever led.

Encouraged, Craig set up a meeting with his boss to update him. He told his boss, "The difference for me with the team this time was changing the nature of the dialogue by asking questions. It worked. I found myself engaging others and listening with curiosity rather than through my judgmental assumptions. Confidentially, I like myself better this way."

Craig's self-esteem and confidence increased. His tendency to have too little *grit* when keeping his word with others shifted to a sincere consideration of others and not letting them down. He put together a matrix of projects and promises, and every day for half an hour reviews what is due, by when, and actions to take.

Let's also consider what changed in the imbalance of his *gravitas*. His arrogance, which reflected his need for self-importance, was replaced by an increased awareness and regard for the importance of what others can contribute. He gained humility and a willingness to listen to others. He accomplished this by facing the negative impact he was having, choosing to take the feedback he was given, and doing the work of building new habits. Craig was able to listen to feedback that was divergent from his self-perceptions and make a choice to see how he could build new habits to be a better leader. He wound up improving his reputation and turning the negative impact he was having into one that was positive and empowering.

Moving beyond the discomforts we experience in receiving feedback, the choice to grow and develop is a gift to ourselves. It provides us with the freedom to activate our potential and evolve. The willingness to face his foibles and flaws allowed Craig to form new habits and transform his approaches, behaviors, the quality of his connection with others, and his demeanor. He succeeded in elevating the substance and quality of his leadership, his presence, and his impact.

Chapter 2
Defining Executive Presence

In this chapter, we examine some of the critical distinctions of executive presence including some of the current myths and misunderstandings about presence. In light of this, we offer perspectives our clients have used to transcend limitations that had been holding them back. We look at what leaders have in common and how and why each leader is unique. We explore the power leaders have to decide what kind of a leader it's important for them to be, and how this strengthens their presence.

Presence is a leader's individual mark or imprimatur

As a leader your presence is your individual mark or imprimatur. It is a major factor in how you and your leadership are perceived, one that directly influences your ability to succeed. Whether through your own aspirations or requests made of you as a result of your organization's performance review process, you can decide the time is right to integrate vital skills and perspectives that bring new depth to your leadership. Doing so will distinguish you and enhance your presence in ways that will be valuable to you and to the men and women you lead.

Think for a moment about your presence. What happens when you walk into a room, lead a meeting, deliver a difficult message? What impact are you actually having? Is it the impact you want to be having? What would you change, and how would you improve if you could?

Your presence is as unique as your fingerprints

As a leader, it is important to remember that your presence is one of a kind. Some of the aspects that are unique about your presence have to do with the values and principles that are important to you. The knowledge and experience you've gained from tough challenges, situations, and risks you've faced also makes your presence unique. There is no one else like you. Your presence is your unique mark upon the world—one that you leave each and every time you interact with people, use your voice, and use your power. While there are different "styles" of leadership (an internet search will show you more than 150,000,000 results) and different leadership theories, you and your leadership presence are unique and one of a kind.

Our research on presence

In our research, we've come across many definitions of executive presence. For example, one definition identifies executive presence as a blending of temperament, competencies, and skills that, when combined, send all the right "signals" (Bates, 2016). Or another definition from Sylvia Ann Hewlett describes executive presence as the "it factor," one that "telegraphs that you are in charge or deserve to be" and that you have the right to be there (Hewlett, 2014).

Our research on leadership presence includes the findings of many of the thought leaders who have contributed to the body of knowledge about leadership and presence. Leadership theories begin with the *Great Man Theory*, written in the 1840s, leading up to the present with writers such as Jim Collins, Peter Drucker, Bill George, Daniel Goleman, Marshall Goldsmith, Frances Hesselbein, Rosabeth Moss Kanter, Jim Kouzes, Barry Posner, Amy Cuddy, Sylvia Ann Hewlett, John Beeson, Sally Helgesen, Erica Ariel Fox, Suzanne Bates, Robert E. Kaplan,

Robert B. Kaiser, Kristi Hedges, and Dr. Gavin R. Dagley, just to name a few.

Dagley's research study in 2013 entitled "Executive Presence: Influence Beyond Authority" asked respondents to give a description of the "first person to come to mind with a positive presence." The study produced major findings about how a positive executive presence was distinguished through effective leadership. These findings verified that effective leadership causes people to act, while effective executive presence causes people to listen. Dagley found that the evaluation-based characteristics that define long-term positive leadership presence are interpersonal behavior patterns, values in action, intellect and expertise, outcome delivery ability, and the use of power.

Leaders sometimes find that they have leadership and executive presence issues through negative feedback that they receive. They hear comments such as "you're too demanding" or "you come across with an arrogance that is putting people off." They are asked by their boss, HR, or board to deal with their issues as developmental opportunities. Amid the complexities involved, the process might begin by undoing the confusion as to how a leader is unknowingly getting in his or her own way. Taking ownership and accountability for what they project and how their negative patterns and behaviors land on the people they lead offers them the opportunity to look more deeply. Here is where leaders take the distinctions of our theory, model, and framework and put them to work. Here is where leaders take it upon themselves to evolve from the inside out, where *grace* becomes their game changer, where their approaches, behaviors, connection with the men and women they lead, and their demeanor begin to reflect the evolution they want for themselves.

Consider that your presence is the essence of what is distinguishing your leadership and is responsible for the quality of the journey toward achieving results. For example, Mary, an executive in a large financial services firm, led people in her division through an extremely difficult period, after which her boss said, "People are complaining about your leadership." Mary responded incredulously, "What do you want—results or happy people?" Her boss looked at her and said, "Mary, the best leaders achieve both."

Mary had the *grit* and the *gravitas* to get through this difficult period, but her team wound up feeling disempowered, drained, and depleted. An exemplary leader would have had a more constructive and positive impact—a knowledge and focus on the importance of his or her team's resilience. This means melding the persistence that comes with *grit* and the know-how that comes from *gravitas* with the *constructive power of grace*. With *grace* a leader can inspire and empower the men and women they lead to face and get through difficult times with the knowledge that they are respected and highly valued for their efforts.

Your leadership and your presence are one. Your presence both forms and communicates the distinguishing characteristics of your leadership. As a leader, you have the choice to be responsible for the quality of your presence and how it impacts people and the processes you lead people through. *How* you lead to reach your objectives matters. *How* you get the men and women you lead "there" matters. Leadership goes hand in hand with challenges. The ability to deal effectively with challenges includes motivating and inspiring people to overcome them. As a leader, how your presence influences successful performance and results depends on all of this and more.

We're going to share some of the issues that leaders grapple with. Before we do, take a few moments to consider the following: Imagine you are interviewing three people who know you well to give you feedback about your leadership:

- *What would they say are your greatest strengths?*
- *What would they say are areas you might improve?*
- *How would they describe your presence?*

Although presence has been thought of as somewhat of an enigma, the impact of a leader's presence is anything but. Observe any leader you've known. You can see the impact of their presence through the approaches they take, through their behavior, through the quality of how they connect with people, and through their demeanor—the positive or negative energy in the way they conduct themselves in general. Consider the following to understand the means through which you impact people through your presence.

The formula is this: **A+B+C+D = IoP**:

Approaches, **B**ehaviors, the quality of **C**onnection with others, and **D**emeanor are what generate the **I**mpact **o**f a leader's **P**resence.

The constructive power of grace is the game changer for elevating the impact of one's presence as a leader. *Grace* is composed of constructive approaches, constructive behaviors, constructive ways of connecting with people, and constructive energy in one's demeanor.

How is your *presence impacting* those you lead and work with?

Your *approaches* convey your attitude and frame of mind, how you feel about what it is you are addressing. This can include the position you take in facing and addressing people and situations. **What can you observe about the approaches you take?**

Your *behaviors* are the actions you take. Your actions reflect your intentions and your values. For instance, it matters when you act with integrity. **What do your behaviors reflect about you?**

The *quality of your connection with people* helps you convey how you want the people around you to feel. Do you want them to feel that they are considered and respected? Do you want them to feel a sense that they are valued? People interpret what they feel in the way someone has connected with them. As Maya Angelou said, "I've learned that people will forget what you said, people will forget what you did, but people will never forget how you made them feel." **What do you want people to feel when you connect with them?**

Your *demeanor* reflects and broadcasts your state of mind and attitude. It is visible whenever you enter a room, have a conversation, attend or participate in a meeting. Your attitudes are visible in your facial expressions, your voice, your body language, whether you are attentive or distracted, agitated or relaxed, ruffled or ready, irritated, impatient, or calm and collected. **Are you aware of what your demeanor reflects to others?**

The impact of your presence is well within your control at every moment. As you integrate *the skills and qualities of grace* into your leadership, your *grit* and *gravitas* become more effective, engagement will increase, your teams will be able to work more productively together, and problems will be solved more innovatively and effectively. As your awareness of the *impact of your presence* increases through your A, B, C, and D, you can cause your presence to evolve.

Here are some of the issues that leaders deal with in their development:

When I walk into a room, I'm told I look junior and not confident, I don't appear calm and collected.

You will find, as you read further, how you can develop and modulate your *grit* and *gravitas* to enhance the way your presence comes across to others. As you do, you will be able to see how to shift your approaches, your behaviors, the quality of your connection with others, and your demeanor so that your presence evolves.

My board is all men, and I have to have a presence they respect. I need to stand my ground/hold my own—my presence has to be a strong one.

Through the distinctions we will cover throughout this book you will understand how to develop your ability to constructively push back, hold, or take ground. As you integrate these skills, you can cause your presence to evolve. This will be evident in the approaches you will take, the behaviors you choose, the quality of how you now connect with others, and the shift in energy of your way of being that is reflected in your demeanor.

I am seen as always in the weeds and too tactical. I need to be perceived as strategic.

What are the differences between being in the weeds versus being strategic? What are the differences in leaders' approaches, behaviors, the quality of how they connect with others, and their demeanor when they are being tactical versus when they are being strategic? In the chapters to follow, you will be able to clearly identify this difference for yourself and elevate the quality of the impact that you have.

When I get in front of an audience, I am afraid to lose them if I'm not engaging enough. I don't have enough confidence in myself or my presence, and I think that gets in the way of what I want to contribute.

What are the ABCD's of a leader who successfully engages an audience? What can be shifted in a leader's approaches, behaviors, the quality of how they connect with others, and the energy of their demeanor that increase their confidence to make the contribution they want to make? In the chapters that follow, you will be able to answer this for yourself.

Common myths of executive presence

A myth is a widely held belief, idea, or story explaining some natural or social phenomenon. There are many myths about presence—who has it, who doesn't, and why—which seem to exclude the idea that you can grow or evolve. As perplexed as people can be about executive presence, people also underestimate their own potential to grow and evolve, no matter how accomplished they are.

Myth 1: *You are born with it or not.*

Executive presence is not about having something

charismatic in your personality that you are born with. Your uniqueness, however, is something you *are* born with, and your unique way of being with people is something within your power to develop and hone, author, and evolve. This includes the quality of how you listen to others, the interest you take in their success, the ways in which you lend your support, communicate, inspire, and bring out the best in those you lead. No one is born with these skills. They are learned. Anyone with a sincere desire can purposefully take ownership of the impact they currently have and evolve from there.

When leaders examine who they are inspired by and engage in a process that defines the kind of leader it's important for them to be, they begin to harness potential they didn't know they had. For example, Rachina thought she was a doer, not someone who could have executive presence. While she recognized her own intelligence, her impact with others came as a shock to her as she leaned into her role with meaningful purpose and intention. She took risks, had a few missteps, but honed her approaches, her behaviors, and the quality of her connection with others as she went along. All of this showed up positively in her demeanor. Her sense of her presence grew through her willingness to risk failing, to try new approaches and behaviors, to trust in her growing ability to connect with people as a leader, and to allow her demeanor to reflect the changes she was embracing.

Myth 2: *If you are an introvert, you can't have executive presence.*

What does the idea of being an introvert mean to you? Many believe without question that if they see themselves as an introvert, they are at a disadvantage in terms of being able to develop a strong executive presence. In fact, people who see themselves as introverts can be the most extraordinary leaders with a calming and reassuring presence. Susan Cain saw herself as an introvert. Her book entitled *Quiet* points out ways that people can go beyond this label. How? Presence can become fueled by your passion to lead and make a difference. In Susan's case, she began to see herself reach beyond her introversion as she adeptly defended one of her clients in a negotiation. She was present in ways she had never been before. This surprising outcome led to her research and the writing of her book. Introverts can have extraordinary leadership capabilities. Their capacity to reflect deeply and develop evidence and logical approaches to ideas and contributions becomes even more valuable through their leadership.

Myth 3: *Presence is all about charisma.*

A dictionary definition of charisma is "compelling attractiveness or charm that can inspire devotion in others." Words infused with common meaning can be misleading, such as another dictionary definition for charisma: "a divinely conferred power or talent."

While many icons can be seen as charismatic, there are also many who made a significant difference through their leadership but would not be considered charismatic. Beyond his meager circumstances, Abraham Lincoln had a humble yet driven force to educate himself, communicate, connect, and help people understand important perspectives. His drive for social justice was embedded in his values, which provided the purpose for his leadership and his impact. He had many challenges to overcome such as occasional depression, resistance to his "shabby look," his failures to succeed, and the numerous naysayers he encountered. His legacy was the result of how his *grit, grace* and *gravitas* came together. His *grit* was the result of his persistence. His *gravitas* took root through the knowledge and experience he forged over the years. He infused them with his *grace*, using the language of inspiration and reason. His leadership and his presence transformed our nation.

Personal investment in shaping executive presence

Many leaders are unaware of how imbalances in their *grit* and/or *gravitas* are negatively impacting those they lead. They are unaware of how their approaches, behaviors, the quality of how they are connecting with people, and their demeanor are causing stressful, undesirable outcomes. Leadership is an enormous responsibility, not just because of the technical and economic demands leaders face, but because they directly impact the quality of people's lives when they are at work—for better or for worse. When things go wrong and leaders lash out reactively, when they impact people in stressful ways, there are negative consequences that affect morale and engagement. These leaders have another option—the option to be transformative rather than reactive. Strengthening what is transformative within you is harder, much harder, at first. But it allows you to evolve your leadership and your presence. It helps you turn down the daily invitations to merely react, to behave without constructive intent, or leave ill will, negativity, and disrespect in your wake. Strengthening what is transformative in you enables you to increase rather than diminish the energizing, empowering aspects of your presence. It will increase your ability to accomplish the results that you and those you lead set out to achieve. By investing your energies in constructive ways, you will build a solid foundation for innovation and success.

On the door to Oprah Winfrey's office is a sign that reads: "Be responsible for the energy you bring into this room." Your energy can be positive, negative, constructive, or destructive. It can lift people up, and it can bring people down. It can bring people together, and it can drive people apart. These are choices you make that show up in the energy of your demeanor and contribute to the impact of your presence.

The engine of *grace* is *constructive power*. It rests on the two pillars of *reaction management* and *relationship intelligence*. When leaders use their *constructive power* to look for solutions and see possibilities, their positive energy is an advantage in overcoming challenges. We've considered some of Dagley's research in terms of defining "positive presence." Later in this book, we will discuss further how exemplary leaders have developed a positive presence that successfully integrates *grit* and *gravitas* with *grace*.

In his research, Dagley also looked into something he termed "dark presence" in answer to the question: "If 'negative' or 'dark presence' is defined as an anxious reaction to a person's presence, who springs to mind as someone with [a] strong negative presence?" We will also look at examples that will provide insight into some of the more difficult dynamics in regard to a "dark" or "negative presence."

Although they may not have started out that way, there are men and women who have successfully done the work that has allowed them to become exemplary leaders. It wasn't because they had charisma. It was because they had a strong and sincere commitment to evolve—no matter their age, no matter their gender. They identified where they were missing the mark, and they invested in understanding and integrating new skills that became evident in their approaches, their behaviors, the quality of their connection with the men and women they lead, and their demeanor. The presence that exemplary leaders reflect are the qualities and skills they learned and integrated into their leadership. The way they led and the quality of their impact changed. They took ownership of the values and behaviors that exemplified their personal leadership ideal.

As your awareness increases you will notice that people feel your presence. Your presence and your leadership are one—your presence is the essence of who you are that comes through how you lead and treat people. As we mentioned earlier, Maya Angelou shared words of wisdom with us all when she said "I've learned that people will forget what you said, what you did, but they will always remember how you made them feel."

The two essential pillars of *grace*

What does grace have to do with increasing executive presence? Exemplary leaders excel in their ability to bring out the best in the men and women they lead. Their *presence* is grounded in the two pillars of *grace, reaction management* and *relationship intelligence.* Both pillars hold the keys to a leader having a solid foundation through which they are able to increase the value of their *grit* and their *gravitas* with the *constructive power of grace.*

The engine of *grace* is *constructive power,* power that results from the discipline of *reaction management* and the wisdom of *relationship intelligence.* Think of *reaction management* as giving you the keys to your development as a leader. Why? Because understanding how to deal effectively with your emotional reactions and the emotional reactions of those you lead allows you to have dominion in extraordinarily effective ways that are not available to you otherwise.

Consider *relationship intelligence* as the home of emotional intelligence. Why? Because everything depends on the quality of your relationships—including the one you have with yourself. *Relationship intelligence* increases your awareness and your self-management, as well as your influence and impact with others. As you integrate and strengthen the skills that come with the application of *constructive power* to transform imbalances in your *grit* and your *gravitas,* your executive presence will evolve.

Relationship intelligence and *reaction management* involve many essential skills we include in the pages to follow. For example, let's take a look at one of the skills you will learn more about: *elevating emotional states.* This involves a leader's ability to *elevate* negative emotionally explosive situations between individuals and team members—*emotional states*—from negative to neutral to positive. Think about the *relationship intelligence* and *reaction management* involved in a leader's ability to *elevate emotional states* when the stakes are high. How can a leader's approaches, behaviors, the quality of the connection with those he or she leads, and demeanor result in his or her team overcoming disappointments and obstacles to do their best while under a great deal of pressure to perform? Pressure can produce adverse reactions in people. Unless skillfully dealt with, innovative thinking and a sense of psychological safety will shut down.

We're going to explore the brain science that deals with why and how innovative thinking shuts down, focus is lost, and engagement decreases when people are in what we call the *"reactive zone."* We will see how a leader can use the skill of *elevating emotional states* to bring people out of the *reactive zone* and increase their effectiveness in dealing with the problems at hand.

The skills of *grace*, as they enhance the value of your *grit* and your *gravitas*, will also transform the quality, energy, and impact of your presence. You can almost always successfully neutralize any of the negativity your presence has held. Using *grace's constructive power* allows you to use your influence in new ways that increase engagement, productivity, and performance.

So what is presence? We've dedicated the last seven years to researching, studying, and defining what presence is. We've developed our methods and models, principles, and approaches to address our clients' needs. We have observed the outcomes they've been able to achieve by putting into practice what they've learned in their work with us. By the time you have finished this book, what you will learn about presence—and specifically your presence—will serve you well. You will have a firm grasp on the qualities that will allow you to evolve as a leader and the actionable skills that increase your value to others in your organization. You will have the ability to elevate your presence in ways that empower you to achieve your goals and help others achieve theirs. The next chapter explores the distinctions of the first pillar of grace—*reaction management.*

Chapter 3
Reaction Management: The First Pillar of *Grace*

In this chapter, we look at the importance of reaction management, one of the two foundational pillars of grace. We examine how the brain deals with emotions and reactions, and how to step out of the reactive zone to regain objectivity and presence of mind. The skills of reaction management enable you to build access to the constructive power of grace.

Reaction management is a pillar of strength in a leader. Why? As a leader, your reactions and the reactions of those you lead, along with their emotional undercurrents, are of vital importance regarding the dynamics of your team and the outcomes they are able to produce. How you handle reactions and emotions determines the impact of your presence and the emotional culture of your organization. On a daily basis your reactions and emotions will influence the quality of performance, the strength of engagement, and the morale of the men and women you lead. Through examples we'll share, along with the skills discussed in this chapter, you'll gain a deeper understanding of how *reaction management* and the presence of mind it gives you, allows you to move beyond the initial negative states of your reactions and address breakdowns through the use of your *constructive power*.

Many of the leaders we have worked with over the past several decades have taken it upon themselves to master the internal and external complexities that leadership development involves. They have sought out personal growth within themselves and accepted the opportunity to evolve the outward expression and impact of their leadership and their presence. One of the critical tasks involved was developing their *reaction management* skills—skills that allowed them to gain the presence of mind to constructively deal with their adverse reactions and the emotions that are a part of them. As they added the *constructive power* of *grace* to their *grit* and their *gravitas*, their approaches, behaviors, the quality of their connection with the men and women they lead, and their demeanor—their way of being—changed for the better. Let's look at some of the science involved.

Many studies of brain science emerging over recent years have proven that the human brain is a social organ. Our physiological and neurological reactions are shaped by social interactions. As Matthew Lieberman, researcher at UCLA, said: "Most processes operating in the background when your brain is at rest are involved in thinking about other people and yourself" (Lieberman, 2013). For leaders, this represents both challenges and opportunities for improving their leadership presence. Leaders who understand the social dynamics within the brain can more effectively develop a productive culture that supports collaborative teamwork and engages their employees' best talents and abilities.

An inheritance we all share

Reactions are built-in design elements of the human experience. They serve as essential signals that originate from our primal brain, the amygdala, whose job is to ensure survival through its fight or flight orientation. Fighting with an enemy or predator or running from some life-threatening form of danger are the amygdala's reactions in the face of anything that poses a threat to our existence.

The human brain as it has evolved has not shed its original function; the amygdala has remained intact even as higher order functions have taken their place within us. This process is both the good news and the bad news. We recognize in an instant that some form of danger or threat is near. However, while we retain the capacities involved in fight or flight, the nature of the threats we experience are more varied. Some are life-threatening, others may be in the social form, as Matthew Lieberman points out. In the social forms we encounter, we can come across people behaving in adverse or destructive ways. In David Rock's article, "SCARF: A brain-based model for collaborating with and influencing others," his research reveals that "much of our motivation driving social behavior is governed by an overarching organizing principle of minimizing threat and maximizing reward" (Gordon, 2008) and that "several domains of social experience draw upon the same brain networks to maximize reward and minimize threat as the brain networks used for primary survival needs" (Lieberman and Eisenberger, 2008). "In other words," David Rock continues, "social needs [protection, safety, etc.] are treated in much the same way as the need for food and water."

The amygdala, reading social situations as threats, helps us understand the emotional undercurrents and undertows of organizational life: Someone behaves disrespectfully, embarrasses you in an important meeting, takes credit for an idea you came up with, or damages your reputation in some irreparable way by the negative feedback he or she gives that is designed to make you less well thought of and themselves better thought of.

Feelings are different than emotions. Emotions originate in one's subconscious. "Emotions play out in the theater of the body while feelings play out in the theater of the mind" (McKay, 2018). Feelings originate in the neocortical regions of the brain, are mental associations and reactions to emotions, and are subjective in being influenced by personal experience, beliefs, and memories. A feeling is a mental portrayal of what is going on in your body when you have an emotion and is a byproduct of your brain perceiving and assigning meaning to the emotion (taken from the readings of neuroscientists Dr. Antonio Demasio, M.D., Ph.D., and Dr. Sarah McKay).

There are so many highly charged situations that take place in the encounters and interactions of everyday life. Look around and you can see countless examples: people "losing it" on the road or parking too close to your car, then screaming and cursing you because you ask them to move so you can open your car door. At times it seems that only a very few mature souls have dominion over their emotions, while others live with emotional outbursts or lashing out in negative ways. They lack the skills to handle the more difficult human emotions constructively. They spend a lot of time in the *reactive zone.*

So what is the *reactive zone*? It is the state that we are in when the amygdala takes over and overrides our higher order thinking. It is the state recognizable by the amygdala's emotional cues signaling danger. What happens to you when you are in the *reactive zone*? It doesn't feel good to be in the reactive zone, and the amygdala's solution is to fight or flee. Our brains are searching for a way to relieve the discomfort, irritation, embarrassment, anxiety, apprehension, or unease we feel when our reactions are in high gear. *Reaction management* helps to bring us to a calmer state. It helps us regain our presence of mind so we can think more clearly. Then, in preparation for addressing the source of the reaction, we can clarify an outcome worth having. In the pages that follow, you will learn skills and methods to increase your ability to manage reactions.

Managing reactions

In your role as a leader, your ability to manage your reactions to situations, especially challenging ones, plays a critical role in your effectiveness and your reputation with those you lead. The *constructive power of grace* provides leaders with the means for dealing with emotions and reactions in ways that can dramatically shorten the time it takes to restore mutual understanding, alignment, and productivity.

Viktor Frankl was an Austrian neurologist and psychiatrist as well as a Holocaust survivor. One of the significant contributions of his work—the ideas and practices of what he called Logotherapy—was founded on the idea that striving to find meaning in life is the primary, most powerfully motivating, driving force in humans. His most famous book, *Man's Search for Meaning,* outlines how his theories helped him survive his Holocaust experience and how that experience further developed and reinforced his ideas. Victor Frankl created this simple equation:

"Between stimulus and response, there is a space. In that space lies our freedom and our power to choose our response. In that response lies our growth and our happiness."

Here is the brain science we all need to know. When the amygdala is engaged, our higher order thinking, which is located in the prefrontal cortex, shuts down. Part of managing our reactions is recognizing that in the space Viktor Frankl describes sometimes we need a little time and self-discipline to process what triggered our reaction. By managing our reactions, we are able to recognize the amygdala in action, see the fight or flight reaction in play, and in that moment between stimulus and response that Viktor Frankl describes, choose our response. Doing so is the equivalent of moving from "one room" in our brain to another. We leave the room where the amygdala beckons us to fight or run away and regain the benefits of the higher level thinking that, by virtue of managing our reaction, is available to us in our prefrontal cortex. Here is where we can call on our *constructive power*.

How valuable would it be to increase your ability and presence of mind to regulate, control, and neutralize negative reactions in the moment they occur? Think of the leaders you know, leaders you have worked for, those who have been the best models and those who have been the worst. What does it look like when *reaction management* is absent in a leader? What changes when a leader has dominion over his or her reactions?

Reaction management & self-awareness

The skills of *reaction management* begin with increasing self-awareness. Self-awareness leads to the presence of mind to notice a reaction is occurring and to focus attention on the message that comes to us in the form of emotions and thoughts.

In building *reaction management* skills, awareness is key. Here are some questions you can ask yourself that increase awareness:

- *Why do I feel threatened?*
- *What happened in the situation that doesn't "sit right"?*
- *What emotions am I feeling?*
- *Are expectations, values, or boundaries involved?*

Asking yourself these questions allows you to tune in to the messages your emotions are sending. Emotions serve an important purpose: to help us become aware when something feels threatening. Think of emotions as part of your internal "navigation system," trying to get your attention. Many people would prefer to avoid emotions that are trying to get their attention. If our emotions weren't valuable to us, we wouldn't have them. They help us zero in on the moment that triggered our reaction. By paying attention to these signals, you can gain control in two ways: 1. You can regain your presence of mind, and 2. You can release the grip of the reaction you are having to what occurred. By pausing to ask yourself questions, you begin to take yourself out of the *reactive zone*. Your state changes from a state of reactivity to one where, as Viktor Frankl tells us, you can choose your response. You can begin to think more clearly, objectively, and strategically about how to constructively deal with the situation at hand.

Think about the most recent thing that triggered a reaction in you. What's the first thing you notice about what happened when you were experiencing a reaction to someone or something? You may have felt an immediate sense of tension or stress. Notice the physical sensations such as tightness in your chest or tension in your neck, back, or jaw, and notice the thoughts, worries, and concern you are left with as a result of this recent occurrence. What emotion was present? For example, was it anger, frustration, impatience, fear, annoyance, or anxiety? Was it a combination of emotions?

Here is an example of what can occur in the *reactive zone* and one leader's ability to stand outside of it.

"Several colleagues and I were conducting a large group process, and during a segment we addressed a critical issue. There was someone in the group whose mindset is usually negative. She kept making it like she wasn't being understood, and her insistence was escalating rather than diminishing. I saw an opening to ask her a question and was able to direct the conversation in a more productive way as a result."

He continued: *"My colleague pulled me aside. He was agitated. He had been in the front of the room during that segment, and he can be very controlling. It felt to me like he wanted to suppress me and make it all about him somehow. It had already been a long day, and I noticed how tired I was feeling. I asked myself, what do I want to expend my energy on? This is a tempest in a teapot."*

Reviewing what had occurred, he added: *"I was aware of a feeling in my chest and thoughts whirling around in my head. While he kept talking at me in an agitated way, I watched myself thinking of options so I could put him in his place. I observed myself reacting to him, and I made a conscious choice. I realized that from time to time he was going to pop off, ride on my back, forget that he is where he is in no small measure because of me, not remember where his opportunity—this opportunity—came from. I let him finish getting his thoughts out. I did not put him in his place. I said, "Ok, hopefully, we can discuss this further."*

Choosing to step out of the reactive zone

The leader in the example above, after regaining his presence of mind, made a choice to step out of the *reactive zone* to find a constructive way to handle his own reactions and deal with his colleague's reactions. Reflecting on the situation, he said the following:

"I know that I would rather pick my spots. I know that I have nothing to prove. But another part of the reaction I was having was a voice in my head vying to put him in his place, accusing me of not being strong because I was choosing not to do so. But what I became aware of is that I want to have a choice, even in the moments when it looks as though I don't have one. While it just takes a moment to shift myself from reaction to awareness, it takes a LOT of discipline. It's worth it. What I wanted was for the outcome to be achieved in the fairest and most equitable way with the right protocols, which need to be relational. Because when the relational part gets thin and the emotional parts get stirred up, that's when everything wants to go into a reaction."

Your presence of mind and your ability to choose your response take you out of the *reactive zone*, prevent negative states from escalating, and progress from derailing. Had one colleague not had the presence of mind to diffuse the initial reaction of the person who insisted she was not being understood, the process could have continued escalating. He also took a moment to choose his response as his colleague's need to control came at him as a heightened agitated reaction. He had the presence of mind to deal with his internal dialogue that wanted to pull him in the direction of putting his colleague "in his place." He was aware of his fatigue, aware of his colleague's tendency to try to control what happens, aware that this reaction his colleague was having was a "tempest in a teapot" to which he could choose not to react. Stepping out of the *reactive zone*, he let his colleague finish talking, and he decided his response. His thoughts continued but he avoided getting stuck in their grip; he used his *constructive power* to deescalate and neutralize the negativity his colleague was expressing.

Let's re-examine the statement: "Between stimulus and response there is a space." This means pressing the pause button so you can notice and identify the stimulus triggering your reaction. At the moment a reaction occurs, notice that there is a change in your state, something akin to going in an instant from calm to agitated. Your heart may beat faster. As emotions such as anger, frustration, or annoyance arise, you will notice a change happening in your sense of alignment and connection with the person or persons you are reacting to. There will seem to be a distance between you, a divide in how you see what is happening around you, a lack of mutual understanding.

Without pressing the pause button, the way you might express your concerns could take the form of criticism or accusation, creating defensiveness on the part of yourself and the other person. Seeking to understand, having the intent to restore understanding, changes the approach and the outcome from one that is based in defenses of who is right or wrong to one where mutual understanding can lead to resolution.

Let's go a little deeper to look at when a reaction leads to accusation and criticism. Think about your intentions in the moment of a reaction. Are you seeking to accuse or understand? Be right or be understood? Are you seeking to resolve or cement a miscommunication or a misunderstanding? What is your intention? Before you speak, ask yourself: What is an outcome worth having? This is the *"freedom and power to choose our response"* that Viktor Frankl describes.

Lastly, he points to the opportunity inherent in having chosen a response that transcends our initial reaction. Frankl tells us that *"here is an opportunity for our growth and happiness."* What does he want us to understand? If you can guide yourself through the disruptive reactions and emotions that occur, if you can increase your self-awareness and the ability to have the presence of mind to regulate and control your reactions in the moment, of what value would this be to you as a leader? *Reaction management* is about gaining mastery in and with our lives and our roles. By releasing the grip of a reaction, you, in effect, re-engage the prefrontal cortex. From there you can call on your *constructive power*; you can provide yourself with a freedom from the reaction and a sound platform for strategic action.

In the example above, our client said he wanted to have a choice even at the moment when it looked to him as if he didn't have one. This was his opportunity to call on the discipline it took to achieve outcomes in the fairest and most equitable way.

Stepping out of the reactive zone

When a reaction is triggered, the amygdala activates and throws us into one of two modes: fight or flight. *Grit* and *gravitas* can do their worst when this happens. Consider how the imbalances of *grit* and *gravitas* escalate in the midst of reactions of fight or flight. With fight and flight, the threat and the emotions that come with it haven't yet been understood. The emotions carry important messages trying to get our attention. With fight and flight, some form of fear, vulnerability, dread, or confusion take hold. This often includes the physical reactions of stress and discomfort in the body. When the emotion isn't yet understood, *grit* and *gravitas* can come through in entitled, insulting, impatient, or intolerant ways, or expressed through some form of avoidance and/or wanting to escape.

For the moment, when a reaction takes over, *grace* is unavailable. The goal in the moment of a reaction is to have a way to become aware of what you are feeling; this is different than judging yourself, someone else, or the reaction you are having. Feeling emotions, rather than denying them or pushing them away, is essential for well-being. When we accept our emotions, we can use them to help us understand why we felt threatened. After restoring our objectivity and presence of mind, we regain a sense of control so we can address the situation from the most constructive intent; we can better understand ourselves and each other. Through the desire we have to restore our balance, we learn from our experience and the emotions that triggered the reaction.

When the amygdala becomes activated, the two operative modes are fight or flight. Let's look at the difference between them. Fight involves outward actions toward others, based in words or something physical such as overturning a desk and punching a wall or verbal attacks such as blaming while pointing a finger, finding fault, and lashing out in some form of anger or resentment.

Flight involves fleeing or withdrawing into oneself in some way. In the face of a reaction, flight is the drive to avoid, escape from what is happening, or withdraw from uncomfortable feelings such as a sense of hopelessness about what is occurring. Flight creates a sense of wanting to disappear, to get away as fast as possible. This is not cowardice; this is an amygdala reaction—the urge to flee and find protection from what feels threatening.

Flight

Kyle is a sales executive, relatively new to his role in a firm with an operationally oriented culture. In preparation for the quarterly executive meeting, Kyle's team prepared the market information and sales projections he needed for the meeting. The team, wanting to make the results seem better than they were and not wanting to admit they were struggling with certain sales and profit results, provided Kyle with projections that were, in fact, too optimistic about the remainder of the year and the year to follow. Trusting in his staff—this approach has always worked well in his previous role—he did not double-check the report he'd received and made the mistake of taking the work at face value. (Here's where Kyle needed work on too little *grit*.) As a result, in the executive meeting Kyle found himself in an uncomfortable, compromised position. From the point of view of the CEO and his peers, he looked as though he wasn't on top of the market trends and lacked control over his team. (Here's where Kyle needed to work on too little *gravitas*.)

In the midst of their criticism, Kyle froze like a deer in the headlights. His initial reaction of flight took hold. He didn't become defensive; he kept his composure outwardly, but inwardly his mind was racing. He shrank back waiting for a break where he could have some privacy to process what had happened. He had to figure out how he and his team could find a way to work more effectively together and ensure nothing like this ever happened again.

Later in a meeting with the CEO, Kyle was further criticized for what had occurred. But the CEO suggested ideas that Kyle could consider in building his team. He valued the considerable capabilities Kyle could bring to the organization and understood that people have to find their way in a new culture.

We'll look at the steps Kyle took a little further on. First, let's examine an example of a fight reaction below. This leader, Allison, had to deal with a change that she did not handle well, one that wreaked havoc with her team and negatively impacted her reputation.

Fight

Allison was a member of a leadership team in charge of sales, marketing, and communications for an insurance company. As an action-oriented driver (*grit*), she also had a great deal of industry knowledge and experience (*gravitas*). Her greatest strengths were in the areas of strategic thinking and innovation. The chief marketing officer reported to her, allowing Allison to concentrate on company strategy. However, without warning, the chief marketing officer resigned. In a panic, Allison realized she didn't have anyone within marketing she could count on to competently handle the role. Even though she was in the midst of working on the company's strategic plan, with the marketing group now leaderless, and knowing about all the work that needed to be done in getting ready for new product launches and the next insurance enrollment period, she jumped into the role herself.

With the extreme overwhelming stress she felt in having taken on the extra role, Allison became reactive in angry and controlling ways. This had a negative impact on her approaches, behaviors, the quality of connection with the people on her team, and her demeanor. Her overly assertive, directive manner came across to both peers and direct reports as rude, judgmental, harsh, and dismissive. (The result of too much *grit* was a negative impact and diminished her value and effectiveness as a leader.) A tipping point occurred in a project meeting when Allison screamed at someone in front of the whole marketing team. After the meeting, members of the team realized they needed help from HR in dealing with their situation.

Allison's reputation shifted from a perception of her as a thoughtful, respectful, and strategic leader to one of severely lacking in self-awareness and emotional intelligence. The manner with which she tried to control her workload and the dismissive and insensitive nature of her behavior served to derail her. She lost the trust of her staff and peers. The imbalances in her *grit* and *gravitas* generated feelings of intimidation, defensiveness, and fear in others around her, which resulted in negatively changing her impact, her presence, and her reputation.

Her boss, the CEO, realized that Allison was under extreme stress by having taken on the strategic plan and the management of marketing. He gave her feedback about the seriousness of her behavioral impact. He offered her the opportunity to have coaching. She needed to mend her relationships and reputation, learn how to better manage her reactions, and become a more effective collaborator, partner, and leader.

Some reactions are harder to transcend

There are times when challenging situations and the impact of difficult or unexpected circumstances can seem to roll off your back so you are able to have the presence of mind you need in a tense moment. Other times, your emotions can seem to "get the better of you" so you have trouble getting out of the *reactive zone*. When the amygdala reacts to a threat taking place and higher cognitive abilities are temporarily out of reach, it is all too easy to feel a loss of control. In the more difficult reactions that occur when things don't roll off your back, there are actions you can take to get yourself out of the *reactive zone*. You can press the pause button, reflect on what happened, and identify the emotions that have been triggered. If you observe your emotions rather than judge them, you will be able to see why this emotion is trying to get your attention. Why do you feel threatened? For example, are you afraid of failing? The goal is to reconnect with your ability to generate a constructive outcome. The steps we outline below help you manage reactions that are more difficult. They shorten the time it takes to tap into your *constructive power* and turn things around. When you experience a reaction:

Step 1: *Press the pause button (create a space between stimulus and response):*

Identify physical sensations. Are you feeling tension? Where is the discomfort? Are you gritting your teeth? Is your stomach in knots? Take a slow breath in and out in each area you've identified. As you breathe, see if you can begin to identify the emotion you are feeling.

In Kyle's case during the meeting with his colleagues that first triggered his reaction, he took stock of where he was feeling the tension in his body. He noticed that his hands were shaking, and he turned his attention to taking slow breaths to calm himself. He realized that he was feeling embarrassed and also exposed. As he breathed into the areas of tension, he felt his hands stop shaking and felt his composure returning.

Step 2: *Release your reaction and identify emotions:*

- Give yourself some privacy where you can work on what we call a *responsible release.*

- On a piece of paper, for your eyes only, write down the reactions you are having. What emotions are trying to get your attention? Are you feeling anger, resentment, fear, anxiety, dread, and so on? You may notice more than one emotion.

- Describe what you are feeling as well as your thoughts and concerns.

When Kyle returned to his office, he asked his administrator to hold his calls for 30 minutes. He closed his door and took out his pad and pen. He put the word "embarrassed" at the top of the page and listed his concerns and thoughts from his experience at the meeting. He then wrote the word "anxiety" and listed his thoughts and concerns that came to his mind about his team and the risks involved with having unwisely trusted them for the information and projections needed for the meeting.

Step 3: Make the most of responsibly releasing a reaction:

- Without judging yourself, allow yourself to become aware of the feelings and thoughts regarding the person or situation you are reacting to. Let them flow freely onto a piece of paper or device. As you express your feelings and thoughts, notice if the reaction is lessening, remaining the same, or increasing. If your reaction is the same or increasing, keep writing. Keep letting yourself write down all of the negative feelings and thoughts that are a part of this reaction.

- Keep going until you feel less and less of a "charge." The charge is an important signal. Writing your *responsible release* in this way empties the negativity onto the page. And when the charge is gone, the page can be torn up and thrown away, having served its purpose.

- When the situation no longer feels charged, you will have brought yourself out of the *reactive zone* to a place where you can *access your constructive power*. You bring yourself to the moment Viktor Frankl describes: the moment where the work you've done to regain your presence of mind allows you to "*choose your response*." You will recognize the moment when you are "there." At that point you can identify an outcome worth having.

Kyle realized that the ease with which he had been able to rely on his previous team did not transfer to this culture. He saw that the expectations in this new company required the kind of grit and rigor expected in an engineering firm. He realized that he needed to work with his team to set up rules of engagement and accountability that would serve them well.

Step 4: What is something you've learned?

Reflect on what you have become aware of and determine the constructive outcome you want in the situation and/or with the person(s) involved and the actions you could take.

Do you see a connection to an imbalance of your *grit* or *gravitas*? For example, Kyle saw that he hadn't doubled-checked the numbers prior to the meeting. This led to a lack of holding his team accountable and made him look like he didn't know what he was doing. What outcomes are worth having? What habits or practices can you put in place that keep you from being triggered into the *reactive zone*? What actions will you take?

Kyle wrote down the outcomes he envisioned that would generate accuracy with projections, and that would come from strengthening his relationship with his team. He then wrote down the reputation he wanted with his peers and the CEO, and the actions he needed to take to accomplish this:

- *Kyle first debriefed with his boss, asking for input he needed to determine how best to work with his team.*
- *He then met with each key peer on the executive*

team to brief them and request their input and their support as he shifted his approach to determining future sales projections.

- *He pulled his staff together to discuss the experience he had at the executive meeting and the outcome he wanted, pointing out each issue and what needed to change.*
- *Kyle worked back through the input he received from his boss and the executive team members, and where his team had not been honest about the performance to date.*
- *The team worked through a plan that Kyle approved, and they understood that he would be holding them accountable.*
- *Kyle and his staff created their rules of engagement, including the kind of straight talk and honesty that would have given the accurate numbers and projections for the meeting.*

While it may seem that it would take a lot of time to go through these steps, it actually winds up taking only a short time—short in comparison to the time and energy it takes to deal with the residual damage if the situation goes unchecked. Situations such as Kyle's can become part of a person's reputation—a defining input in how people think of them.

Here are the critical tasks of *reaction management*

that make the biggest difference. A *responsible release* of a reaction is not about lashing out in anger, hurling accusations, gossiping behind someone's back, shaming them publicly, or putting them in their place even though in the midst of a reaction you might feel like doing that! A *responsible release* is one in which, with *grace,* you look to get yourself to a place where you are more aware and have gained an understanding of what triggered your reaction. For example, you understand why you felt threatened, pressured, or hopeless. Identifying your emotions and the trigger without judging yourself begins to restore your equanimity and your presence of mind.

Once you've moved past the amygdala's primal urge for fight or flight, you'll notice that you've regained access to the prefrontal cortex where higher order thinking is available to you so you can generate a constructive outcome that addresses this negative situation.

Train yourself to recognize when you are in the *reactive zone* so you can regain your objectivity and *presence of mind* before you do or say anything. Train yourself to take effective measures to resolve what triggered the reaction. Train yourself to use the skills and qualities of *grace* to modulate imbalances in your *grit* and *gravitas*. Leaders who can't do this risk becoming a liability to themselves, their team, their stakeholders, and their organization as a whole. Leaders whose reactions go unchecked, whose *grit* and *gravitas* are given free rein in fueling their reactions, damage relationships and their reputations. They generate a brand that shows while their results are important, there are negative consequences to the drama and difficulty their leadership creates.

The skills of *reaction management* are the keys to the kingdom. For leadership there is nothing more important than dominion over how you behave day to day, and how you behave when things are at their worst.

Now let's move on to the second pillar of *grace,* **relationship intelligence.**

GRACE

Grace rests on the two pillars of Reaction Management and Relationship Intelligence:

REACTION MANAGEMENT

Reaction Management provides a leader with knowledge that impacts his or her ability to move more quickly beyond the negative states of reactions. A leader is then able to access the brain's remarkable capacity to see and take constructive approaches; approaches that resolve and remove barriers to achieving desired results.

RELATIONSHIP INTELLIGENCE

Relationship Intelligence provides a leader with knowledge of emotions, how and why they effect people and their performance, and the skills involved in elevating emotional operating states from negative to neutral to positive. With its roots in brain science and emotional intelligence, Relationship Intelligence provides critical knowledge for bringing out the best in people and empowering them when it matters most.

© 2019 Jane Firth and Andrea Zintz www.gritgracegravitas.com

Chapter 4
The Second Pillar of *Grace*: Relationship Intelligence

The second pillar of grace is relationship intelligence. In this chapter, we begin to explore the combined constructive power of reaction management, which we covered in the last chapter, and relationship intelligence, which we begin to address in this chapter and explore further in the chapter that follows.

Relationship intelligence begins with your awareness of the relationship you have with yourself. The way you *relate* to yourself directly influences how you *relate* to others. And how the people you lead relate to one another has more to do with your level of self-awareness than you may realize. Something of great value takes place when you maximize your ability to relate to yourself and others through your *constructive power*. It turns out that what holds purpose and meaning for you, what we call your *highest leadership aspirations*, are an essential part of your *internal bearings*. This is your inner compass that you can use to navigate toward your evolution as a leader.

But first, given that we all have our foibles and flaws, we need to make it safe to see where our behaviors, approaches, the quality of how we relate to ourselves and how we connect with others, and our demeanor are lacking the considerable benefits our *constructive power* makes possible. For instance, the more you increase your ability to evaluate and adjust the imbalances in your *grit* and *gravitas* the more aware you become of how they have been getting in your way. You will more easily identify patterns that aren't working for you. Understanding your reactions and patterns allows you to press the "edit/undo" button and replace the patterns that don't work for you.

In the pages that follow, you'll find examples of leaders who have gone through the process of identifying how they were getting in their own way, how they came to understand the negative patterns of their *grit* and their *gravitas*, and how they found the words to define their *internal leadership bearings*.

Our first example is Robert, a leader who did not

get a role he very much wanted. Our second example, Stan, is someone who was elevated to a global position with senior VP status. Our third is Anna, who struggled with inequities she encountered in her organization.

Robert's wake-up call

Robert, a regional director for a telecommunications company, was responsible for operations and sales for his part of the business. He actively pursued coaching to develop himself as a more effective leader. As part of his work on his leadership skills, he took the opportunity to consider his *grit* and his *gravitas* in light of his current approaches, behaviors, connection with people, and his demeanor —for instance, his pattern of coming across as overconfident and self-assured. To understand the impact he was currently having as a leader, Robert reviewed the definitions of *grit* and *gravitas* and took notes regarding the times he saw himself behaving with either too much or too little *grit* and the times he behaved with too much or too little *gravitas*. He also included the feedback and advice he obtained from a previous 360 assessment from his manager, peers, and the men and women he led. He tied this information to what he was seeing about his *grit* and his *gravitas*. Reflecting in this way led him to become more aware of his strengths and re-energize his desire to have a more senior executive role. But before he had taken steps to integrate what he was learning, he was presented with an opportunity.

The CEO of the company, having identified Robert as a person with valuable talent and leadership skills, tapped him as a strong candidate for a position that had opened on the senior leadership team. Requested to interview as the lead candidate for this position, Robert felt certain he would be chosen. However, in his certainty that this would be easy, he reverted to his pattern of overconfidence. This came through in the three interviews he faced with the CEO, the Human Resources SVP, and a seasoned senior leadership team member. During the interviews, Robert's pattern of being overly self-assured was perceived as lacking thoughtfulness and depth. He came across to the interviewers as arrogant. The consensus of the three executives was that his answers seemed superficial and his demeanor lacked the qualities they needed as a member of the senior leadership team. The CEO chose someone else for the role.

Discouraged and disheartened, Robert wrestled with his reactions and emotions. At first the options he saw were either fight or flight in nature: He considered leaving the company, he wrestled with his anger and disappointment with the sense he'd been treated unfairly, and he viewed the chosen candidate as having less merit than himself.

This initial reaction was followed by a period of trying to better understand what had led him to lose this opportunity he very much wanted. Taking responsibility for what had occurred, Robert came to realize that by relying on his sense of overconfidence he had derailed this opportunity.

For Robert, this experience was an important wake-up call. He decided that instead of leaving the company where he had been very successful, he would work to turn things around in his current role. He turned his efforts toward integrating the skills and qualities of *grace* into his leadership. As part of this work, we led him through a process that began with the following question: *What kind of leader is it important for me to be? Why does this matter?* In answering this question, Robert reflected on leaders he had admired over the years. He looked very carefully at what had impressed him about how they led: their approaches, their behaviors, the quality of their connection with people, and what he'd noticed about their demeanor. He asked himself what kind of influence he wanted to be able to have should another opportunity to join the senior leadership team become available to him. He considered the qualities that would allow him to be a more positive influence with his peers and the men and women he leads. He looked at changes he could make that would allow him to be a more effective leader when challenges and difficult problems arose.

Robert took the opportunity to make important changes in his leadership, a decision not every leader would choose to make. But when a leader does make this choice, what motivates him or her to do so? Some of the motivations that have been shared with us are included in the following: For some, it is a wake-up call of one sort or another; for others, it may start out with wanting to be a part of, or a catalyst for, something that makes for a more meaningful and fulfilling life. Still others have a sense that they want greater peace of mind and the ability to empower themselves in the face of troubling situations they are not in control of. But at the moment of choice there is always a kind of coming to terms with their situation, a deeper reflection that results in a leader's very personal answers to essential questions.

What kind of leader is it important for me to be? Why does this matter?

Leaders who are aspiring to develop themselves know that every single one of us is flawed. But they don't stop there. They don't hide behind this knowledge or pretend that it isn't the case. They are driven to be better and to do better. They ask more of themselves. They want to face their flaws head-on because they know they can't change what they haven't owned and taken responsibility for. They face their flaws not to tear themselves down, but to allow themselves to grow and evolve.

Robert's wake-up call came when he did not get the position he had wanted on the senior leadership team. After he dealt with his initial reactions, he wanted to understand why he was not chosen, figure out what was getting in his way, and what to do about it. He suspected, and rightly so as he came to find out, that he was getting in his *own* way. That was good news to him because he knew that if he was the problem, there was something he could do about it. After dealing with his initial reactions following that disappointing outcome, he determined to continue putting himself in the running for advancement.

As we say in the beginning of this chapter, *relationship intelligence* begins with the way you relate to yourself, which directly influences how you relate to others. As you increase this aspect of your *relationship intelligence,* you will become more readily aware of your motivations, of the triggers that set off negative reactions, and of the patterns you then default to that get in your way. In Robert's case, in addition to what he discovered about the interviews, he looked at his leadership in general, facing his foibles and flaws as a leader. He recognized imbalances where too much *grit* and *gravitas* on his part obscured his perspective when it came to the opportunity to empower others. His default pattern was: "*I have to drive things myself. I have the answers, and I have to make the decisions.*" Rather than being focused on empowering his direct reports, he defaulted to powering workload demands through himself, not realizing he was robbing others of the opportunity to grow and contribute. This pattern also resulted in Robert not providing clear direction to his team, creating confusion with regard to his priorities.

Looking at the imbalances in his *grit* and *gravitas*, he could see his foibles and flaws in a more clear and constructive way. Having raised his awareness, here are some of the observations he became aware of:

"*I can see that I've been overly focused on my stature and making an impression. I am too focused on my own ideas and getting results. I haven't been thoughtful enough to listen to others and their ideas. I am not relaxed in the sense that I can be overly intense and overbearing. I need to trust and empower my direct reports and partners more. I can give so much direction that it winds up being confusing. I need to be more focused on key objectives and vision and trust my people to achieve the results."*

With these observations and his new awareness, Robert could be more objective as to what had caused him to lose the opportunity to serve on the senior leadership team. The imbalances he saw in his *grit* and *gravitas* led him to understand how his approach, behavior, the quality of how he connected with the interviewers, and his demeanor had reflected a careless overconfidence. He saw how this had him read the situation inaccurately beforehand—and make a poor decision as to how to present himself that cost him the opportunity. As he dealt with his initial negative reactions, he was able to go beyond them. He was able to recognize how he was getting in his own way. He used this as a wake-up call and as a catalyst for his evolution as a leader.

Let's look at another example. Stan had the opportunity to move from a VP level leader of a single division to a larger global role at the Senior VP level. While Robert's situation was driven by a failure to achieve an important goal, Stan had a natural inclination toward the idea of becoming exemplary as a leader. His new role had a wider scope of leadership responsibility. Stan became responsible for three new divisions with sites throughout North America, Europe, Latin America, and Asia, tripling the number of direct reports under his watch.

Stan's desire to be an exemplary leader

Stan considered his default patterns; he looked at them in light of what would be expected of him in this new role and environment. He saw that it would require him to develop additional leadership skills, skills that would allow him to address the complexities and design structures that would be needed to achieve results. Further, Stan identified additional leadership skills he would need to interface successfully with the various microcultures involved in this complex environment.

Working together with us, he asked himself questions such as: *"What will this require of me as a leader? What skills will I need?"*

Addressing his default patterns and the imbalances of his *grit* and *gravitas*, Stan became aware of the tendencies he had that could be a problem in his new role. For instance, an imbalance in his *gravitas* was his desire to ensure his peers and employees understood everything including all possible risks. One of his default patterns was to go way overboard in his explanations. In trying to share his extensive knowledge and expertise, he would go on and on with his explanations; in trying to be crystal clear, he would say far too much and talk for far too long. Because he is highly respected, people have tolerated his tendency of being overly verbose and pedantic.

In his reflections, Stan saw other examples of default patterns, such as his reluctance to ask for support. Part of *grit* is a leader's comfort level with his or her power, which includes the ability to delegate and invite collaboration and support. He recognized that this imbalance in his *grit* was motivated by his concern for not imposing on anyone. This is one of the ways leaders manifest their discomfort with power.

Stan also recognized that he had an aversion to systematic approaches—approaches that are more organized and methodical than his current ones. As he considered the meaning he placed behind the idea of flexibility, he saw how he had been confused about the idea that structures get in the way of being flexible. Stan realized that flexibility needs to coexist with organization and structure; it wasn't a matter of one or the other. He also saw how the unintended consequences of his default pattern could interfere with efficiency, effectiveness, and progress in how he leads. Stan considered proactive ways to correct these imbalances in his *grit*, learning that he can still be flexible in his thought process while setting up systems that will insure consistency and cross-functionally coordinated efforts.

Knowing he wanted to be exemplary, Stan faced his foibles and flaws so he could determine the best development plan for himself as a leader. Beginning this process, he reflected on the question: *What kind of leader is it important for me to be, and why?* He reflected on the leaders he had admired over the years. He looked very carefully at what had impressed him about how they led, what he observed in their approaches, their behaviors, the quality of their connection with people, and their demeanor. He asked himself what kind of impact he wanted to be able to have with his new stakeholders, and with the men and women he would now lead. He considered what would allow him to be an exemplary leader when there were challenges and when there were hard problems to solve. What would he need to pay attention to in order to increase his *reaction management* skills and his *relationship intelligence*?

Stan was anxious to define and embrace his

highest leadership aspirations and found great energy from the way this helped clarify his internal bearings. Examining the imbalances in his grit and gravitas, Stan took an honest look at his foibles and flaws. In support of his desire to be exemplary, he noticed where his own approaches, behaviors, connections with his team and stakeholders, and his demeanor were placing obstacles in his path to achieving his leadership development goals. He was successful in defining what mattered most to him at this important time in his career. He defined his internal bearings to reflect the meaningful contributions he wanted to make through his highest leadership aspirations.

One way to distinguish the difference between our first two examples, Robert and Stan, is to notice what motivated each of them to engage in the process of their leadership development. For both, the opportunity to evolve held meaning. For Robert, it was a wake-up call. For Stan, it was the enlarged scope of leadership responsibilities that came with a promotion. Our next example, Anna, was also motivated by the desire to evolve; hers was driven by the inequities in her organization that she kept coming up against, and the stress she was experiencing as a result. On the one hand, the inequities she encountered could be seen as a disadvantage, but on the other hand, she could assess the toll they were taking and shift her focus to one that would allow her to re-energize and empower herself.

Anna and William were partners in a financial services firm they had started together. Their firm was acquired by a larger global financial services corporation. One of the persistent challenges Anna faced in the new larger firm was what appeared to be an exclusive "good old boys club." One example is how this group of men shared among themselves the larger client opportunities that arose. Notwithstanding Anna's gravitas and her considerable professional competence and expertise, these client opportunities were not extended to her. Bringing this dilemma to William's attention did nothing to alleviate the situation. He was unable to empathize with her; he was enjoying this advantage he had in the new culture, and in their discussions together he defended the rationale for why the clients were offered to him. He was happy with the recognition and status he had gained along with the bonus and benefits that came with it at year end.

Speaking to William only added to the frustration and stress Anna was experiencing. She realized she could not turn to William to help her resolve the situation as she might have in the past. Anna saw the need to find another way to resolve her stress and frustration.

Anna takes stock

As we worked together, Anna saw that she had choices in the matter. She took an honest look at the frustration, resentment, and anger she had been feeling over the situation and the cost to her energy and well-being; she realized the extensive inequity of the situation and the disempowering effect it was having on her life. Fighting the situation would continue to be exhausting. It would place her in an adversarial position and detract from her ability to focus and build value for her clients.

Taking stock of it all at this important time in her life, she assessed and evaluated the results she had achieved year after year; she got in touch with the extraordinary commitment she had to her clients and their success; and she recognized in no uncertain terms how dedicated she was—and had been throughout her career. Seeing all of this, she decided to forge her own path forward. She put into words her *highest leadership aspirations*; once her *internal bearings* were in place, she was able to harness the *constructive power of grace* for herself. She was able to face the inequities she'd been dealing with more objectively without her *grit* being filled with bitterness and resentment. She let go of the frustration and anger and took back her power; she felt empowered by recognizing her own value—not in an arrogant way—but in a grounded and meaningful way. She was able to understand and own the depth and breadth of her *gravitas* with a deeper level of respect from within. She began to focus her energies in a different way.

Keeping her *internal bearings* present, Anna was able to re-energize and empower herself. No longer disempowered by the reactions she had to the built-in bias of the culture, her grasp of her *higher aspirations* shifted the way she focused and utilized her energy and expertise. Her stress levels decreased, her results increased and, with the changes that were reflected in her approaches, behaviors, the quality of her connection with people, and her demeanor, her presence in the organization began to be recognized and appreciated in new and important ways.

Review

Relationship intelligence begins with the internal relationship you have with yourself. Defining your *internal bearings* begins with a deeply personal exploration. Your *highest leadership aspirations* are the result of reflection that helps you define your higher purpose as a leader, contributions that hold meaning for you in answering the question: *What kind of leader is it important for me to be, and why?* Your *highest aspirations* reflect what matters most to you in your life. They are essential elements of your *internal bearings*.

Keeping your internal bearings present

> You can't go back and change the beginning, but you can start where you are and change the ending.
> C. S. Lewis

When you keep your *internal bearings* present, for example, reading them over each day, they *anchor* you to your higher purpose. Your *internal bearings* are your purpose, guide, and compass all rolled into one. Allow yourself to absorb the energy and inspiration you've put into words. They lead you to recognize where and with whom you can bring about constructive progress that otherwise would not have been possible. The meaning, empowerment, and inspiration of your *internal bearings* and your *highest leadership aspirations* are the energizing fuel that help you accomplish what matters most to you.

The following are some examples of aspirations our clients have identified:

- *To keep our mission present so that we are, as a team, able to be inspired by how, both individually and collectively, we are making our vision come to life in the day to day of our work, and over the long term.*

- *As a leader, I am committed to bringing out the best from the members of my team. I want to be known as a leader who generates group trust, alignment, and collaboration. I want to shift my tendency to work with individuals and become adept at getting the best performance from and with the team.*

- *To engage with my direct reports in ways that inspire their energy and engagement by not solving their problems for them, as I have done in the past. Instead, I strengthen my ability to invite their ideas and solutions; I express my confidence in their abilities to solve, innovate, and execute effectively.*

- *To continuously pursue the improvement of my strategic thinking by learning through my experiences—both successes and challenges—and by taking responsible risks that elevate my wisdom and choices as a leader.*

- *To be attentive to providing valuable guidance and strategic advice I can offer the organization by communicating with my stakeholders in a way that is relatable, commercially reasonable, creative, forward-thinking, and based on high integrity.*

- *To develop a greater strength in recognizing and developing talent. As a leader, I'm committed to helping the organization continue to evolve and stay ahead of the competition. I will identify and develop the next generation of leaders that will be seen as part of the "commercial team" and as "true partners."*

When you are reading another's *leadership aspirations*, remember that they hold meaning and energy for their author. By identifying your *highest leadership aspirations*, you will find you are inspired and energized by your words. The positive energy and inspiration you feel confirms that you have gotten to the heart of what matters to you as a leader.

Chapter 5
Relationship Intelligence: Leadership & the Social Brain

In this chapter, we will look at relationship intelligence through an outward facing lens toward a deeper knowledge of human dynamics in organizational settings. We'll explore neuroscientific research focused on what we can learn about the way the brain reacts in social settings. We will examine distinctions that clue us in to how the social brain impacts the dynamics between people in groups and teams, how these dynamics either block or facilitate teamwork, performance, and progress, and how a leader can use this information to leverage the benefits of their constructive power.

The impact you have as a leader is the determining factor of the culture you generate, whether you are leading the entire organization, a division, a geographic territory, or a project team. In

Chapter 4, we introduced *relationship intelligence* from the perspective of having the most empowering relationship with yourself and your leadership by identifying your *highest leadership aspirations*. These form the basis of your *internal bearings*, which allow your leadership to be guided and shaped by what matters most at this important time. Remember, if you have already begun to define your *highest leadership aspirations* and created the foundation of your *internal bearings*, by keeping them present and leading from them, your leadership will evolve.

Let's consider the *relationship intelligence* offered to us through the social brain as it affects our sensitivities to the dynamics taking place in social interactions in organizational settings. Many studies of brain science emerging over recent years have proven that the human brain is a social organ, that our physiological and neurological reactions are shaped by our social interactions. The social brain is a source of invisible cues when social interactions are taking place. Recent scientific discoveries find that in the brain the amygdala is not just on the lookout for danger. It also searches for cues and clues that help us in building our social connections. It provides us with intelligence for building our social bonds and working to sustain our relationships over time. How? The social brain helps us look for safe connections. Can this person be trusted? Is this group one I feel comfortable with, one I want to be a part of? The social brain scans our social interactions; its highest goal is to be able to find evidence that translates to "We are close, we are safe, we share a future" (Daniel Coyle, 2018).

As a leader, it is important to pay special attention to the evidence that social bonds matter more than we might realize. Consider the following:

In the longest longitudinal study ever conducted, the Harvard Study of Adult Development, researchers have followed the lives of more than 600 people for over 75 years—from the 1930s up to the present time—and what they have found is that the most important element in any one of us having a happy and fulfilling life rests on the nature, quality, and reliability of our relationships. The good life, it turns out, is built with good relationships. In their 75-year study, they found that toxic relationships are bad for health, worse than divorce. Consider that people spend a tremendous amount of their lives at work. As a leader, every day you have the opportunity to ensure that people's lives are made better by virtue of the culture you create and the way your approaches, behaviors, the quality of your connection with people, and your demeanor can foster a constructive influence on the quality of relationships at work. For more about the Harvard Study of Adult Development, we recommend the TED Talk entitled "What makes a good life? Lessons from the longest study on happiness." The link is listed in the Resources section at the back of this book.

What does the social brain tell us about needs?

The major finding in the Harvard Study of Adult Development provides us with the insight that what matters most are positive relationships. As we said in the beginning of this chapter, your leadership serves as the determining factor of the quality of the culture itself. The values you engender in the culture have a direct impact on how the people you lead relate to each other and the norms for interpersonal behavior. When you understand the social dynamics going on within the brain, you can more effectively engage your employees' best talents, support their collaborative synergy and teamwork, and use the *relationship intelligence* you've gained to ensure that the men and women you lead feel considered, respected, and safe.

As we said earlier, the human brain is a social organ through which our physiological and neurological reactions are shaped by our social interactions. As we saw with *reaction management* in

Chapter 3, when we look into a moment when we are having a reaction, we can notice our amygdala is signaling a threat. A person or situation has triggered the fight or flight reaction we are experiencing. But we have a choice to make our thoughts stand still, identify the emotion we are experiencing, and recognize the need that is being thwarted or blocked. This reflection allows us to work with our reactions rather than default only to our assumptions such as who is right or wrong or who is to blame; we can find a place within ourselves to generate a constructive resolution to the situation at hand.

As a leader, you can draw on your *constructive power* to listen to others with this knowledge in mind and support others in constructively resolving challenging situations. Consider, then, why does the quality of social interactions matter to the achievement of outcomes? What does this tell us about how leaders shape culture to build their teams, foster engagement and alignment, and bring people together with purpose, meaning, and a sense of belonging? For leaders, increased knowledge of the social brain allows valuable insights that can be drawn upon to enhance key relationships and understand the needs of your team as individuals as well as a group.

The social brain and psychological safety

Let's examine one of the key elements for putting *relationship intelligence* into action—creating the conditions for trust. An aspect of what generates trust is when your approaches, behaviors, the quality of connection with the men and women you lead, and your demeanor create the conditions that generate a phenomenon called psychological safety. What is psychological safety?

Psychological safety was first explored in a book published in 1965 written by Edgar Schein and Warren Bennis at the Massachusetts Institute of Technology. During that time, they used the term psychological safety to address the need for employees to cope with uncertainty and anxiety in organizational change. Since that time, other social researchers, including Amy Edmondson of Harvard, have built on that premise, expanding the term psychological safety to include the experience of trust and respect at work. Feeling safe depends in large measure upon this concept of the social brain. Research has shed light on how leaders can set the conditions that invite and sustain psychological safety.

Think of a leader you felt or feel comfortable with when speaking up, particularly when you see an idea that can be important to the success of a project or that leaves you with concerns about the project's chances for success. Next, think of a leader around whom you would hesitate to speak out or share your opinion. What is it that makes you hesitate to speak? We have seen many leaders with considerable *gravitas*—deep knowledge in their field—who value their own thoughts and opinions over those of the men and women on their team. Often these leaders have a habit of correcting and putting down team members who speak up, reinforcing a pattern that it is not safe. As Amy Edmondson found, "...if a boss responds with anger or disdain as soon as someone steps forward to speak up about a problem, the safety will quickly evaporate" (Edmondson 2019, p. 157). Psychological safety is critical for the establishment of trust in a group or organization.

The constructive power of grace helps leaders meet the needs of the social brain, in particular, the social needs of the men and women they lead. For that purpose, we turn now to our BETA Model. We created the model below as a guide to understanding and providing for the social needs of groups and teams, for generating the social conditions that translate into *Belonging, Empowerment, Trust,* and *Alignment.* Based on research of the social brain and human needs at work, this model touches on specific dynamics that can result in a culture that invites people to be and do their best, to feel a sense of being part of something meaningful and important, something that makes them feel, as we mentioned earlier, "we are close, we are safe, we share a future." Let's look at the BETA Model and see how the *constructive power of grace* provides for the social brain's needs and the conditions that foster an environment where cooperation and collaboration lead to high performance.

BETA MODEL

The social brain: meaningful engagement, unlocking potential, psychological safety...

Belonging	Empowerment	Trust	Alignment
CREATING THE CONDITIONS FOR SHARED MEANING AND PURPOSE	CREATING THE CONDITIONS FOR LEVERAGING POTENTIAL, AND ENGAGEMENT	CREATING THE CONDITIONS FOR PSYCHOLOGICAL SAFETY	CREATING THE CONDITIONS FOR MAKING SENSE OF THINGS TOGETHER
Inclusion and acceptance	Non-judgmental listening and asking constructive questions that facilitates resolution of challenges	Generous listening and understanding neutralizing negativity	Constructive focus, attention, and efforts, "Can do", "We'll figure this out" approaches
Keeping the door open; being available in general on a consistent basis	Recognizing each team member's value and importance in achieving goals	Being trustworthy and dependable, keeping promises	All-in regarding the team's shared vision, mission and purpose
Approaches that take social needs into consideration	Recognizing and developing the potential, skills, and talent of the people on the team	Fairness with due consideration for differences, diversity, and individual needs.	Flexibility, cooperation, and a spirit of collaborative partnering in evaluating and taking risks
A purpose and mission that people are proud to be a part of	Conflict and/or failure handled in a constructive way; remembering that when things go wrong, we can learn from them	Honesty, integrity, authenticity, and sincerity	Clearly defined direction, goals and responsibilities
Respect and regard for other's perspectives	Ensuring each member of the team has the resources needed to succeed	Compassion for vulnerabilities, including one's own	Putting agreed upon measures and accountabilities in place
All for one, one for all: Shared appreciation for the team's contributions and accomplishments	Advocacy and support team members where and when it matters	Support, cooperation, compromise and forgiveness	Approaching team challenges constructively; rules of engagement and shared values
Keeping vision, mission, and purpose present and active	Bringing objectivity and empathy to disagreements and disruptions	Owning one's responsibility and expressing apology	Putting platforms, structures, resources in place to ensure success

© 2019, 2020 Jane Firth and Andrea Zintz

How to use the BETA Model to diagnose

Belonging, Empowerment, Trust, and *Alignment* are foundational conditions for high performing teams. When issues and problems arise with your team, how can you zero in on the root causes of the matter? Many of the root causes of team dysfunction can be attributed to one or more of the elements within the BETA Model. It is structured to help you identify areas of compromise affecting your team's productivity, engagement, and progress. Here are steps that can serve as a guide in using the model:

1. Consider the situation the team is facing. Scan each column to help you identify elements that may be contributing to the situation. What might be at the core of where and why cooperation and communication are breaking down?

- Scan the columns. In relationship to the situation you are dealing with, which elements catch your attention?
- Ask yourself questions, such as the ones below, that will further clarify each element you've identified. For example, looking at the conditions for:
    - *Belonging* in column one: Is someone on

your team feeling out of the loop or not included?

- *Empowerment* in column two: Does someone on your team lack the resources they need?

- *Trust* in column three: Is someone on your team feeling that the work is not being handled fairly or that they're not receiving due consideration for their contribution?

- *Alignment* in column four: Is someone on your team lacking clear direction, goals, or responsibilities?

2. Check in with yourself: Am I providing the conditions for *Belonging, Empowerment, Trust,* and *Alignment*? For example:

- *Have I been available?*

- *Am I listening generously and objectively?*

- *Am I creating psychological safety?*

- *Am I being clear in my directions and expectations?*

3. Take a few minutes with yourself to consider the following questions:

- *What steps would help address the elements*

I've identified?

- *What can I do differently to create the conditions for psychological safety and generate honest dialogue with my team members?*

- *What is an optimal outcome, and how can I create a constructive approach to get us there?*

As you become familiar with the aspects of the BETA Model, you will begin to see how best to put these distinctions into action. Remember: Every leader is unique, and every leader will differ in terms of how they approach and address particular situations and circumstances that arise within their teams. But your work toward gaining the combined benefits of the two pillars of *grace—reaction management* and *relationship intelligence*—will serve you well in your ability to address any imbalances in *grit* and *gravitas* that have been problematic as well as to access and utilize your *constructive power* to achieve the best possible results with your team.

Now let's pull the curtain back to see how two leaders worked with their teams to establish the conditions outlined in the BETA Model. We'll start with Amber, our youngest exemplary leader.

Amber interviewed for the position of vice

president to lead a team. This team had gone through significant problems with the leader Amber was replacing. Having been hired for the role, Amber took steps in talking with HR to gain an in-depth understanding of each of her direct reports. She was able to gather important perspectives and information and understand what the last few years had been like for each person on her team. In our discussions, Amber shared the following:

"After I'd been hired, the head of HR and I had some important discussions about the team I would be leading, and in these discussions he clued me in; he gave me insight into each of the people on my team. He helped me understand what had taken place and why there had been so many difficulties."

Based on this helpful information, Amber recognized how building *Trust* would serve the team she was about to inherit. To create the conditions for psychological safety, she saw that when she had an opportunity to speak in person with her direct reports, it would be important to listen in a way that would help her gain understanding and be able to neutralize any negativity that had developed over the prior years.

"As I began to get to know each member of my team, I found the information the HR partner had

given me to be very helpful. It allowed me to see the potential in each member of my team and gave me a head start in thinking about how they could each be developed."

Amber saw the importance of creating the conditions for *Empowerment* that would allow her to develop the potential of each team member and inspire their engagement. As Amber shared the approaches she used in getting started with her team, she told us the following:

"I felt it was important to keep in mind that I came from outside the system to lead people who had been through a tough couple of years. I knew it was important to me not to just 'barge in.' I took time with each of them to talk about their expectations and hesitations and understand what they were looking for in a leader. They had concerns such as: Would I be able to understand the work that they did? How would I deal with the fact that they didn't feel like a team? They were on the lookout to see what I did: Would I listen first or just change things? How would I represent them to the higher levels of leadership within the organization? Was I a leader who would value each of them? Could they trust me?"

Amber paid close attention to what her team members had to say, providing a quality of listening that energized, restored a sense of trust, and reset their expectations, opening the door for each of them to be successful. She recognized their need for *Trust* and *Belonging*. Amber continued:

"Almost immediately, they let me know that their interactions with me were very different from the way they had been dealt with over the last few years. I took time to meet with each of them individually as well as together, and I asked them to tell me: 'What do you do in your role? Tell me about it.' And then I shared some of my strengths and experiences with them and what I could provide. Then I asked: 'What do you need from me? What would add value coming from me?' One of my direct reports let me know that she cared about having interesting work; she wanted to take on projects that offered her a challenge and a chance to grow. Later on, she shared with me that through these conversations she felt like she was empowered to grow and contribute for the first time in a long time. I felt really good about that."

Amber recognized the importance of understanding the needs of her direct reports. She saw the importance of developing the conditions for *Belonging*, for generating a sense of being a part of something meaningful together. As Daniel Coyle says, "Group performance depends on behavior that communicates one powerful overarching idea: 'we are safe and connected.'" Amber wanted an approach that would help these discussions feel respectful and safe. By asking questions in the spirit of seeking to understand, she hoped her approach would engender a sense of relatedness through her sincere consideration of their needs. She sought to develop a mutual appreciation for each other's roles and contributions. Amber added:

"My team had been through a great deal. They had felt out of the loop. I shared with them that information and transparency mattered to me. 'Everything I can share with you, I will. Trust me; if there is something I can't share I will have your backs. I will go to bat for each of you; I will go to bat for our team.'"

Amber conveyed consideration, respect, empathy, and compassion toward those she led. She let them know they could trust and rely upon her. She expressed her commitment to creating *Alignment* with her team. She was determined to set the conditions for values and practices they could share. She hoped her promises would ensure a sense that she was someone they could trust and count on to have their best interests at heart. By letting the team know that she had "their backs," she sincerely pledged her advocacy and support, which also set the conditions for their *Empowerment*.

Vulnerability and trust

Amber took the risk of being vulnerable with her team.

"In all the conversations I had with my team, I found myself in a moment where I took a big risk. I said to my team: 'There is a lot you know that I don't. I will do the best I can, but I will make mistakes. Please have patience with me. I want us to be a team.' Somehow showing my own vulnerability helped my team members feel safe in sharing their feelings with me. I did let them know that, as a leader, I was in charge.... I told them: 'I want, and I

> Vulnerability doesn't come after trust—it precedes it. Leaping into the unknown, when done alongside others, causes the solid ground of trust to materialize beneath our feet.
> Daniel Coyle, 2018, p. 107

value, your perspectives. At the end of the day you can count on me to make the decisions.'"

As we mentioned earlier, every leader is unique. As a leader, what would you do, or what have you done, to have your team trust that you have their backs, to have them know that they are valued, and that their needs are considered? How do you create psychological safety? How do you create a sense of belonging to something meaningful and inspiring? "A mere hint of belonging is not enough; one or two signals are not enough. We are built to require lots of signaling, over and over. This is why a sense of belonging is easy to destroy and hard to build" (Coyle, 2018).

Whether you are starting your first leadership opportunity or you are a seasoned leader in your field, your influence and impact make the difference between a dysfunctional team and culture and the conditions in which team members feel a sense of *Belonging, Empowerment, Trust,* and *Alignment*. Your approaches and behaviors toward your team, and the quality of your connection with them, as well as your demeanor, make the defining difference in members of your team knowing they are valued, feel inspired and engaged with you and each other, and motivated toward a shared purpose and meaningful goals.

Our second example illustrates how a leader used the BETA Model to facilitate a group of individual contributors so that they could become a high performing team.

Promoted to a vice president position within a

large construction company, Wayne successfully advanced up the career ladder based on his knowledge, skills, and experience with all facets of construction, along with a prowess for bringing in sales. Considered smart and thoughtful with sound opinions and a thorough understanding of the market, Wayne and his contributions were highly valuable. He was offered his VP position without having had leadership experience.

After Wayne had a 360 assessment with his key stakeholders, his assessment feedback indicated some areas for development including his tendency to be disorganized. Wayne's approach to getting things done was, in his words, *"overly adaptable and flexible,"* which caused his stakeholders uncertainty. Wayne's imbalance in *grit* had him be disorganized and resistant to using structures and systematic approaches. Wayne also had the *imbalance* in his *grit* in terms of avoiding confrontations and delivering difficult feedback to others when needed. This resulted in having his stakeholders concerned regarding his ability to hold his followers accountable. Wayne completed his worksheet on his *Internal Bearings,* which gave him a structure for distinguishing and clarifying what matters most for him as a leader. Based on his highest aspirations, values, and goals, his *internal bearings* gave him a strong foundation for his leadership style. His review of his foibles and flaws allowed him to see merit in his recent 360 observations. He decided to focus his development plan on building a high performing team under his leadership.

Using the BETA Model, Wayne realized that his focus on his production would have to shift to facilitating the productivity of others. Since he preferred maintaining harmony in relationships, he was hesitant to let others know when they didn't meet his expectations. In building *Trust,* Wayne wanted his direct reports to feel a sense of psychological safety and *Belonging,* which would set the conditions for giving and receiving feedback, healthy conflict, and engagement, as well as taking calculated risks. By setting the conditions for *Empowerment,* he would be better able to promote skill development. He saw how developing the conditions for the team's *Alignment* would help him to provide supporting processes and structures, along with accountability for results.

Wayne sat in on some of the team meetings to observe the performance and characteristics of those who would be reporting to him. He also asked the former team leader and other stakeholders of the team about their perceptions of the team's performance. In doing so, he learned that there was an inconsistency in being responsive to stakeholder requests and concerns. He could also see that each direct report tended toward operating independently rather than as a team.

Another part of Wayne's strategy was to foster a connection with his team members; he decided to meet with his direct reports one on one to get to know them better, understand what motivated them, and learn what they found challenging both in their roles and within the group. One of his strengths was *listening to understand*, which, as described in the BETA Model, is an element of setting the conditions for *Trust*. With confidence, Wayne asked questions and shared some of his own experiences. One of the practical insights Wayne came away with from his one-on-one discussions was that his team would value weekly meetings with clear agendas.

How does a leader inspire individuals who are used to operating independently and transform them from individuals to members of a team? To this end, Wayne put a great deal of thought into his first kick-off team meeting, organizing an agenda that would build *Trust*. He opened the meeting with an engaging exercise. After a lively discussion about their experiences and the opportunity to learn things they hadn't known about each other, Wayne let them know more about himself and what his team could expect as well as count on him for. He shared the vision he had for them in becoming a team and his belief in the strength of keeping their mission present to inspire their work together. He then opened the discussion to establish the conditions for building *Trust* as a team.

Wayne asked them to write down one simple action—something they could practice with one another—that would increase their mutual trust throughout the coming month. He provided an example that they could use in making their commitment or customize one of their own. His example was: *"When an issue with a team member arises, instead of listening only to my own assumptions and defaulting to my habit of working independently, I will ask questions to better connect and understand others' perspectives and ideas."*

In his development, Wayne found it challenging to hold people accountable. In correcting this imbalance in his *grit*, he thought of ways to make accountability more user-friendly. Wayne did this by asking the members of the team to pair up with someone else in the group. They put a simple structure in place to talk and debrief monthly. This structure was useful in building their accountability.

In a brief email follow-up, Wayne sought feedback from each member of the team. This helped him resolve the imbalance in his *grit*—his reluctance to request and give feedback. In their feedback, everyone said they enjoyed the meeting and felt they were on the path to becoming a high functioning team. As the weeks went by, it was obvious that the work Wayne and his team had done to think things through together had succeeded in bringing them into *Alignment* and developing the basis for *Trust*.

Using the BETA Model to develop high performance

For the planned meeting the following month, Wayne sent the group an agenda, which included the critical topic of customer service. He began with a lively team exercise by requesting each team member to reflect on times they had a positive experience with a client service representative and times when they had a negative experience. As Wayne worked on setting the conditions for *Alignment*, the discussion prompted the team to make sense of things together. They looked at the lack of structure, processes, and practices in the department, and they saw the benefits they could have in creating them.

Wayne then facilitated a team discussion to arrive at a group vision, one that would build a strong reputation with their stakeholders. The team then looked at ways to structure consistent approaches. They brainstormed measures of success for driving the consistency of customer service. Wayne observed the increase in energy that everyone, including himself, was feeling.

He finished the meeting with the same request as the first meeting, for a simple individual commitment to a behavior that would serve to improve their customer service during the coming month, one that could become sustainable as a habit. Wayne requested they each choose a different accountability buddy than they had before to provide them with support and feedback at least once during the month. The consistency of supporting each other in this way and their growing appreciation for each other's roles and efforts contributed to a sense of *Belonging*.

Now let's turn to how you can use the BETA Model to elevate the emotional operating states of those you lead.

Using the BETA Model to elevate emotional states when there is a lack of engagement

An emotional state of mind can be negative, neutral, or positive. When people do not feel a sense of *Belonging, Empowerment, Trust,* or *Alignment,* their emotional state will be affected. Each member of the team could have a different reaction based on unmet BETA needs.

The elevation of an emotional state of mind happens when social issues and concerns are addressed and resolved. You can use the BETA Model to look for social needs that aren't being met and help eliminate the stressful effects that may be occurring. You might find a decrease in productivity, engagement, *Trust*, or the inability to reach *Alignment* on important decisions. A negative emotional state in a team can be elevated and resolved. A trusted leader can use his or her *constructive power* by asking questions with a sincere desire to understand through empathy and compassion. Try the following process:

1. Address and acknowledge that there is an issue. For instance, you could say: "We seem to be out of *Alignment*, and I want us to get back on track. What do you think has taken us out of *Alignment* with each other?"

2. Establish a condition for attentive listening. Set a ground rule to have each person share their perspective completely before another takes their turn in sharing their perspective.

3. After each person has an opportunity to fully

express their concerns, mirror back what you hear to be sure you've got the essence of what they are expressing, and ensure they know you've understood their perspective.

    a. Ask each person: "Is there anything else? Am I missing anything?"

    b. Thank them for taking the risk of being honest.

4. Make sure each person has the opportunity to share their perspective, which you mirror back, including steps a. and b.

Using the BETA Model, and based on the perspectives they shared with you, what social needs are not being met and should be addressed?

What follows is an example applying the BETA Model to a team. Maybe a member of your team expressed they've felt excluded from important conversations or perhaps several team members feel they are overburdened by their workload and lack sufficient resources they need to accomplish their goals. Although there may be no immediate way to provide the necessary resources, when people feel heard and respected there is an opening to work concerns through together.

When social issues are allowed to remain unresolved, your team is operating in a negative emotional state. When this happens it compromises collaboration, cooperation, and morale in ways that negatively impact productivity, performance, and results. As a leader, you can neutralize this negative state and elevate it to a positive one, restoring social needs that weren't being met and reestablishing cooperative collaboration.

How NOT to elevate emotional states of mind and stay stuck in the reactive zone (*of course, you'd never do these things!*)

1. Harbor ill feelings toward your team members that you complain about to others, rather than directly with the person or persons involved. That way the situation will remain unresolved.

2. Blame members of your team for everything that's going wrong. This way they'll know they're not in your good graces.

3. Only listen to the perspectives of those you like or those who will agree with you. This sets up an excellent barrier to prevent honest communication and equitable outcomes from taking place.

4. Be intimidating in a way that makes it difficult for team members to come to you with their concerns.

5. Have your "busy-ness" take center stage in

your priorities.

6. Have your demeanor communicate your superiority and importance such as: "I have more important things to do than listen to you. Just get your job done. That's what you're being paid for."

7. Hold people accountable in a judgmental way. Criticize them, point out their faults, hold them at arm's length and, by all means, withhold acknowledgment for anything they've done correctly. After all, this is what you expect them to do.

8. Make people feel that expressing emotions is weak or just plain wrong!

As you look at the BETA Model, what might be the right questions to ask? As you reflect on the social needs not being met, what conversations would serve to reestablish the sense of *Belonging* or *Empowerment* or *Trust* or *Alignment* that has become compromised? For example, if someone isn't feeling empowered, what happened? Team members may be feeling they were not treated fairly, not recognized for their contribution, or not supported when support was something they needed. When triggered by these social situations, emotions involved may be frustration, worry, resentment, anger, anxiety, or fear. Feeling heard and understood begins to shift and elevate the emotional state. When leaders ask questions in a sincere and caring way, it invites a feeling of safety in which an honest conversation can lead to resolution. Using your *constructive power*, you can get to the heart of the matter of what took place and together resolve the situation.

The work you are doing to increase your *relationship intelligence* in terms of your team and their social needs helps you use the *constructive power of grace*. You can be a calm facilitator, listening generously, coming across as supportive rather than judgmental, to reach satisfying resolutions when issues arise. This approach shortens the time lost to a negative emotional state. Asking questions with authentic concern and curiosity creates the psychological safety needed for *Trust*. Questions open communication with the power to elevate a negative emotional state that has compromised your team. Doing so, you will neutralize negativity and restore an operating state that is positive and productive.

Summary

The BETA Model helps to define the direction to take in creating resolution and ensuring conditions for *Belonging, Empowerment, Trust,* and *Alignment* with your team. In the present and the future, when you have integrated the *constructive power* available in the two pillars of *grace*, you will be able to bring out the best in people today and leave people better off for having known and worked with you in the future. As your *relationship intelligence* increases, you will become more adept at setting the conditions for high performance, high engagement, and high morale, even when the going gets tough. You will provide those you lead with the fulfillment of being a part of something meaningful together—something that is literally at the heart of the matter in being human and organizing our lives to make a difference. Each element of the BETA Model engages your constructive power to meet the needs of your team.

Chapter 6
The Impact
of Leadership on Culture

In Chapter 5, we looked at the social brain and the BETA Model and how these two elements apply to leading teams. In this chapter, as a way of further increasing an understanding of relationship intelignce, we broaden our view to include some of the ways a leader's role impacts organizational culture and influences other levels of the organization. We look more closely at executive presence as it impacts people, performance, and outcomes.

Using and leveraging
the power of *grit, grace* and *gravitas*

When a leader's efforts include the *constructive power of grace* and the knowledge of the social brain, the culture can benefit greatly. We will explore some of the negative consequences that occur in a culture when this is not the case, where imbalances in *grit* and *gravitas* are normalized. The culture of an organization is the result of the way a leader *leads*. In this chapter, as we explore how different leaders influence the quality and norms of their culture, we'll use the following definition: Culture is composed of the values and behaviors that contribute to the unique social and psychological environment of an organization.

A leader's approaches, behaviors, the quality of their connection with people, and their demeanor powerfully influence the social and psychological environment that distinguishes the culture of their organization. How the leader leads *is* the way people come to understand the rules of engagement and the values that are in play. In other words, it's a matter of what is acceptable and what is not. This is how behaviors become normalized in a culture.

Leadership: A choice to be made and its impact in shaping a culture

When a leader takes the helm, there is a critical choice to be made. Some of our exemplary leaders noted in previous chapters, as well as other leaders we'll meet in this chapter, have chosen to use their *constructive power*. They have intentionally created cultural conditions that could meet the needs of their teams, their key peer relationships, and their stakeholders. They successfully built more collaborative, cross-functional relationships and created the conditions where people felt safe to raise ideas, have difficult conversations, and solve challenges. As a result, silos and egos and win/lose survival patterns gave way to cooperative norms that reinforced a sense of pride, allowing people to feel "we are all in this together." The most successful leaders intentionally set out to create a culture where the conditions for achieving a sense of *Belonging, Empowerment, Trust,* and *Alignment* bring about high performance. They set the stage for people to be and do their best, feel a sense of appreciation and respect for each other, and take pride in the mission they are undertaking together.

Let's contrast this positive leadership approach toward a culture with one we describe as "political." In more political cultures, sustained negative emotional operating states often create costly negative consequences. The decrease in the conditions that meet the social brain's need for connection—for *Belonging, Empowerment, Trust,* and *Alignment*—creates win/lose survival patterns and triggers emotions such as anxiety, resentment, and fear, which exact a toll on productivity, engagement, and morale. Unlike the quality of attention and focus that occur when BETA conditions prevail in a culture, negative, adverse conditions compromise people's ability to focus at higher levels of innovative and objective thinking. The quality of people's attention becomes compromised by the concerns that people have to deal with when they don't feel safe, when the sense of threat engages the amygdala and shuts down their higher order functions.

What common triggers and reactions might employees find themselves dealing with? Leaders can be blind to the compromises they are creating, and to the ways in which a lack of empathy may stifle high performance. Clients have shared experiences of anxious feelings, as if having to walk on eggshells, or a feeling of being excluded or held at arm's length, or thinking they are not valued or respected, or worrying that they've lost their status or importance. Also, in many of these cases, there is a negative impact on people's health and well-being. In a negative political culture where a leader lacks empathy, the employees are deprived of the compassion that is part of a healthy work environment. Empathy is the capacity to feel and understand what another is experiencing. Compassion is the ability to be aware of another's distress accompanied by the desire to alleviate it.

> Empathic workplaces tend to enjoy stronger collaboration, less stress, and greater morale, and their employees will bounce back more quickly from difficult moments such as layoffs.
>
> Jamil Zaki

Healthy competitive cultures operate with integrity and have values-based rules of engagement. When employees have to take risks and put their all into an effort that could have a win or lose outcome, when they lose they don't ignore the lesson—they learn. As a result, they increase their resilience and resolve and become more effective.

Toxic cultures produce negative outcomes. Let's consider some of the research:

- "Positive culture is a vital aspect of running a business—more than 50 percent of executives say corporate culture influences productivity, creativity, profitability, firm value, and growth rates" (Forbes, 2015, taken from research conducted by Duke University's Fuqua School of Business that surveyed more than 1,400 North American CEOs and CFOs over 13 months and concluded: "Overwhelmingly, the executives said that healthy corporate culture is essential for a culture to thrive").

- Ninety-two percent of CEOs reported their organization is empathetic (Forbes, 2018). However, only 50 percent of employees say their CEO is empathetic. This gap in perspective directly impacts employee morale—81 percent of employees would be willing to work longer hours if they felt their employer was empathetic.

- Sixty-one percent of workers say they're burned out in their current job, and 31 percent report high levels of work stress. (CareerBuilder.com, 2017). According to a recent survey, 85 percent of CEOs and CFOs believe that an unhealthy corporate culture leads to unethical behavior (J. R. Graham, C. R. Harvey, J. Popadek, et al., "Corporate Culture: Evidence from the Field," working paper 23255, National Bureau of Economic Research, Cambridge, MA, March 2017).

Often the negative dynamics in a culture are the result of leaders who lack transparency, which normalizes negative behaviors and obscures deception and unfair practices in play. Every leader has the opportunity to design the culture of their group, their organization, their division, and their team. How would you answer questions such as the following?

- *What norms, values, and guidelines and what rules of engagement would best support the people I am leading, the organization itself, and the accomplishment of our strategy and goals?*

- *How do I inspire teamwork—collaboration, synergy, and alignment—that would lead us to create breakthroughs in solving the challenges that we face?*

> People are the common denominator of progress; no improvement is possible with unimproved people.
> John Kenneth Galbraith

What is a leader's role in creating a culture? Leaders express their values and establish norms and patterns through their approaches, behaviors, the quality of their connection with people, and their demeanor. When a leader or group of leaders do not consciously attend to the quality of the culture, imbalances with *grit* and *gravitas* can disrupt the conditions that the social brain seeks for connection. As we said above, leaders model values and establish norms and patterns of interpersonal dynamics through their approaches, behaviors, the quality of their connections with people, and their demeanor. In these ways, leaders communicate what is and isn't considered acceptable, generating the values and norms that people absorb and use in *their* approaches and behaviors and how *they* relate to others in the organization. When a leader lacks the *constructive power of grace,* he or she sets the stage for toxic political dynamics to become normative in a culture.

How does the presence or absence of the *constructive power of grace* and the imbalances of *grit* and *gravitas* contribute to political norms?

Foibles and flaws can be benign and within the normal range. But there are men and women whose use of power as leaders—namely, whose approaches, behaviors, connection with others, and demeanor—fall outside of the normal range to, as they say in *Star Wars*, "the dark side." You can look at the imbalances in *grit* and *gravitas* to understand the misuse of power in more benign ways and also in destructive ways that describe the impact when the *constructive power of grace* is missing.

Here are some examples to consider in terms of imbalances of *grit*:

- ***Close-minded, dug in:*** With too much *grit*, someone can be inflexible, rigid, dug in, stubborn, and exhibit an inability to consider the merits of other perspectives. Someone who comes across in this way tends to lack an inclination for cooperation and to value others for their input and information, especially if they don't agree with their thinking. They may also tend to operate from an investment in their assumptions without verifying their validity.

- ***Dominating, controlling, my way or the highway:*** Behaving in a domineering, demanding, insistent, or inconsiderate manner; others experience this kind of person as controlling. This aspect in someone often has a commanding influence on others, at times using ultimatums, making their dissatisfaction apparent, and indicating others will either conform to his or her desires or else be excluded. Others can experience this element in someone's *grit* as dismissive, demeaning, and disrespectful.

- *Micromanaging, not empowering others:* Someone who micromanages others exercises excessive control and involvement in the details. Rather than empower others, this type of imbalance causes someone to be inclined to either breathe down people's necks or "do it myself to get it done right." A consequence of this imbalance in someone's *grit* is the lack of talent development and the withholding of information and opportunity.

- ***Blaming and judgmental:*** Someone with this tendency is often dominated by their internal negative criticizer that is judging and criticizing themselves and others in disempowering ways. They abdicate their power and responsibility to address matters at hand in a constructive way. They use judgments and criticism to find fault, be right, and justified in place of a desire to restore a more open, objective, and collaborative connection; they are often impatient and irritated.

- ***Oppositional, confrontational, and combative:*** Someone with these imbalances in their *grit* takes an interpersonal approach that is openly competitive and focused on winning at all costs. Sometimes they use below-the-belt tactics to diminish or discredit others and achieve an advantage. These behaviors can be experienced as aggressive and disruptive, resulting in short- and/or long-term consequences. They obstruct progress, create disunity, and leave ill will, distrust, and resentment in their wake.

Too little *grit* can look like:

- ***Ambivalent and conflicted, lacking the ability to select priorities and be decisive:*** Someone with this imbalance in their *grit* has trouble making decisions in a timely way. Their fear of making a wrong decision leaves them confused and ambivalent. The fear of failing causes overthinking and overanalyzing and gets in the way of choosing priorities and making strategic decisions.

- ***Lack of clarity when giving or receiving directions and setting expectations:*** Someone with this imbalance in their *grit,* on the one hand, doesn't set clear priorities or ensure that others have the information they need to execute plans and next steps. On the other hand, when receiving directions and the expectations involved, they don't always clarify because they don't want to feel or look stupid or be perceived as annoying by asking questions.

- ***Discomfort with power, one's own and others':*** When someone has this imbalance in their *grit*, they feel uncomfortable with their own power and with the power others have. They may feel intimidated or lack confidence. Reluctant to stand up for themselves, they may be too eager to please and not want to make waves. Not wanting to impose on others, they bend over backwards; they take on too little or too much in tasks or projects, they don't push back in moments that matter, and they don't set boundaries. This leaves them feeling overwhelmed and burdened, which can lead to burnout.

- ***Difficulty holding others accountable:*** Someone with this imbalance in their *grit* avoids the discomfort of confronting someone who isn't meeting expectations or coming through as agreed. They may avoid having difficult conversations because they don't want to seem demanding; they may confuse the importance of holding people accountable with being seen as overbearing. They often have a fear of conflict and an aversion to contentious dialogue with people who have difficulty being held accountable. Examples include people who act like the victim, people who become defensive and righteous and always have reasons for why things are the way they are, and mercurial people who refuse to be pinned down to what is, in fact, their responsibility.

- ***Avoiding difficult conversations and emotionally charged situations:*** Someone with this imbalance in their *grit* lacks skills for understanding emotions, reactions, and how to approach them constructively. Without these skills, he or she lacks the ability and confidence to access their emotions. Situations such as these trigger a threat rather than opportunity. Without relationship intelligence skills, suppressed feelings can generate reactions expressed in unconstructive ways. The consequence often leads to misunderstandings and blocked progress.

- ***Inconsistent behavior with a consequential effect of seeming or actually being unreliable:*** Someone with this imbalance in their *grit* lacks focus—they often lose the thread of where they are headed. They may have a pattern of showing up late for appointments and meetings, not holding up their end, not following through or keeping their word, which causes doubts as to their dependability and trustworthiness. They often find justifications for their behavior such as "being too busy." They can sound cavalier, as if they lack concern and regard for others.

- ***Disorganized and lacking structures:*** Someone with this imbalance in their *grit* resists using structured and systematic approaches. Their imbalance can result in becoming disorganized and overwhelmed by keeping everything they have to do in their head. They resist using systems, for example, on their computer or journal to help them prioritize, complete tasks, and reach deadlines. Often their office can be messy and disorganized with files piled high on every surface. People with this imbalance in their *grit* have a pattern of creating chaos and causing confusion for themselves and others. They create obstacles that increase difficulty in getting work done.

Here are some examples to consider regarding imbalances of too much *gravitas*:

- ***Hubris, expressing opinions with an air of superiority:*** Because of their considerable experience and expertise, someone with this imbalance in their *gravitas* often dominates conversations in what feels like a condescending manner. Without realizing it, they speak with a careless lack of humility. Their arrogance causes them to correct and criticize others and come across with an air of superiority. Collaborating, cooperating, or functioning as a constructive member of a team can seem unimportant to them in situations where they believe they have superior knowledge and experience.

- ***Thinking one's opinion is the only one that matters:*** Someone with this imbalance in their *gravitas* often goes on and on seeming pedantic, speaking only on "send" and not listening to "receive." Someone with this tendency talks over others and interrupts; they can exhibit an automatic pattern of selective listening. They seem to ignore, minimize, or invalidate the importance of what others have to say. These tendencies prevent them from recognizing the value inherent in listening to the perspectives, opinions, and inputs that others have to contribute. The value of others' ideas is lost. Another consequence is that people can be left frustrated, potentially resentful, and disengaged.

- ***Needing to be the center of attention, stealing or hogging the spotlight:*** Someone with this imbalance in their *gravitas* is overly concerned with their own desires, needs, or interests. They make sure they are the center of attention. They may take all the credit for work that others have contributed to or originated.

- ***Acting in an obstructive and controlling manner:*** Someone with this imbalance in their *gravitas* makes it more challenging to accomplish what needs to be done. Their controlling behavior interferes with and obstructs the flow of progress, using justifications such as "I'm just being a devil's advocate." They delay progress and decision making in unconstructive ways.

- ***Gravitas others perceive as unapproachable and intimidating:*** While it's not the person or expert's intent, sometimes someone with *gravitas* in their field or profession can be regarded as intimidating and unapproachable because of their considerable knowledge when, in fact, they may be shy and introverted. Someone with this imbalance in their *gravitas* may lack the skills that would allow them to be more connected and at ease in collaborating with their teammates and colleagues. Unlike someone who lauds their knowledge over people, these are people who, because of their shyness and introversion, wind up isolated and excluded. One unintended consequence of their not being seen as approachable is the loss of the valuable contributions their considerable knowledge could bring to light.

- ***Inflating one's gravitas competitively at the expense of creating synergy with others:*** Using one's *gravitas* to assert and protect one's status as a source of value above others while directly or indirectly diminishing what others bring to the table. Rather than operating as if "we are better together," someone with this imbalance in their *gravitas* defaults to competitive power plays. In order to keep threats at bay, someone with this imbalance in their *gravitas* keeps others at a distance and at a disadvantage by withholding time, attention, support, cooperation, inclusion, resources, and recognition. The consequences of this behavior are the loss of blended *gravitas* and the potential for synergistic problem solving, breakthrough thinking and innovative progress. An additional consequence is the loss of connection and engagement by others who feel offended.

Too little *gravitas* can look like:

- **Unclaimed *gravitas*, coming across to others as a lack in strength, stature, and significance:** Unlike humility, which down-plays *recognized* abilities, unclaimed *gravitas* reflects an inability or a reticence to adequately recognize one's depth of knowledge and experience. Someone with this imbalance in their *gravitas* robs themselves of the quiet confidence, credibility, and stature that comes from authentically recognizing their *gravitas*. Some of the repercussions can take the form of being discounted, passed over, disregarded, or excluded.

- **An absence of internal permission to own**

one's power and influence:** Someone with this imbalance in their *gravitas* has a lack of confidence in their knowledge and experience, which results in an imbalance in their *grit*—the reluctance to push back, take a stand, or contribute an idea, a perspective, or an observation that could be of value to the matters at hand. The imbalance of one's *gravitas* reflects an absence of internal permission to express one's power and influence. It is all too easy for someone with this imbalance to minimize their accomplishments, their growth, and their development. Their self-confidence suffers as a result. Retreating from important and meaningful opportunities, their lack of confidence impedes or blocks their progress and gets in the way of achieving their considerable potential. As a result, they take on too little; they play too small.

- **Overcompensating, trying too hard to be seen as credible:** Someone with this imbalance in their *gravitas* often tries to prove their value and worthiness. In their efforts to be perceived as capable and credible, they often take on more than they can handle. They also try too hard to be liked and accepted. Someone with this imbalance in their *gravitas* may accept responsibilities without understanding how to build the appropriate platforms and garner the necessary advocacy, resources, and support they need to succeed. To mask their insecurities, they often present a patina of confidence; they overcompensate for a lack of authentic confidence in themselves, which has them appear inauthentic to others.

- **Lacking strategic thinking skills or lacking vision:** Someone with this imbalance in their *gravitas* loses their grasp of the big picture. Their analytic brilliance often has them get caught up in the details. Having zoomed in to analyze the details, they find themselves unable to zoom back out again to see the connections and possibilities that can lead to breakthroughs, innovation, and growth.

As you read the above, what did you notice or recognize about the imbalances in *grit* and *gravitas*? While the foibles and flaws described above could be within the normal range, they're not in a culture that is negatively political. We all have known leaders whose use of power and whose approaches, behaviors, connection with others, and demeanor fell outside of the normal range. To better understand the misuses of power, you can consider the imbalances in *grit* and *gravitas* above and the dynamics that contribute to normalizing politics in organizational cultures.

Imbalances in *grit* and *gravitas* are more common in the absence of BETA conditions

When a leader knowingly or unknowingly allows a political culture to emerge, it permits negative elements to dominate. Without the BETA conditions that fulfill the social needs of employees, the imbalances in *grit* and *gravitas* can leave people stranded in emotional operating states where they may feel angry, anxious, frustrated, fearful, or resentful. The absence of BETA conditions then results in a decrease in morale and collaborative engagement. While some will try their best to work around the lack of collaboration and support, others will disengage in some form or another.

Does the absence of BETA conditions give rise to politics or do politics contribute to the breakdown of the conditions for *Belonging, Empowerment, Trust,* and *Alignment?*

Negative politics is one of the byproducts of a leader's impact on culture. Manipulations, deceptions, unfair practices to influence a result, and competitive behavior between interest groups are all obstacles to cooperation, collaboration, and fair play. They obstruct efforts to come together to achieve common goals successfully.

How do you change norms and behaviors? How do you ensure the conditions that allow for a culture to provide BETA needs? How do you use the *constructive power of grace* to change a culture? In our next chapter, we'll look at two leaders who successfully accomplished this for their organizations.

Chapter 7
Changing a Culture With the Constructive Power of *Grace*

In this chapter, we look at the challenges involved in how two leaders successfully shifted the dynamics of their organization's culture. Culture change can have a positive impact on individuals, teams, and the organization as a whole. How do you move an organization from one emotional operating state to another? How do you move away from dynamics, habits, and processes that aren't working and shift the culture to establish conditions that support employees to flourish and excel? Both of the leaders we'll meet in this chapter drew on the constructive power of grace to change their culture. Let's examine each of their approaches.

Our first example focuses on a leader who engaged members of his organization in a process to establish an inspiring new vision. He was able to elevate the conditions for new norms and behaviors that brought about success in achieving their vision.

Franklin was the CEO of a company we'll call Pharma Bio Technologies. Aware of the obstacles and challenges of the current company culture, Franklin realized transformative change was necessary. He saw that if they kept the status quo, they would not be able to create a flexible, agile, innovative culture and, as a result, not maximize their ability to capitalize on critical opportunities in their market. He wanted to attract the best talent and have a culture that the best of the best would be drawn to; he wanted to design a process that would change and elevate the quality and effectiveness of their culture.

Recognizing the importance of his role as CEO, Franklin saw the need to shift the way the company was performing in a critical segment of their market. He was aware of the problems that were part of the culture of the company, such as a lack of respect between leaders and their employees, a tendency to work in silos, and a sales process and other systems that didn't work with their new market segment. He also saw a lack of inclusiveness for collaboration and too few race and gender contributions. Something had to change. Franklin wanted to build the kind of culture that would significantly increase engagement, collaboration, and success in production, sales, and distribution to meet the needs of their stakeholders and customers. Franklin said, *"I wanted to examine, challenge, and define the 'unwritten rules' of the culture. I needed the leaders on my board to join me in creating an opportunity to develop skills organization-wide that meet the needs of our employees so they can better work together in a cohesive and collaborative way. We knew we had to address barriers in our current culture to achieve this very important outcome."*

Franklin convinced his board to form a culture development committee that could assist in crafting a vision for the new culture that would support the outward-facing vision for the company. He brought onto the committee employees from across the company by level, race, gender, and function. This "Culture Committee" was a model representative of the larger vision for the culture. Using the *constructive power of grace,* his attention to social needs and the components of BETA played an essential role in changing the culture.

The committee was charged with creating subcommittees and initial action plans for rolling out the new culture and developing a vehicle to build the process. During their first meeting they set the conditions for psychological safety so everyone would feel they could express their opinions about what was wrong with the current culture and what needed to change. They also worked together on the vision for the new culture. Franklin set the conditions for alignment. In their process, group members argued and worked through determining the words that captured the right meaning, something they could each own and support. As part of the process, an honest dialogue that included many difficult conversations resulted in a set of rules for engagement. The following lessons emerged.

They saw the need to:

- Value all contributors
- Integrate the culture change into daily business practices
- Remove the barriers to full employee involvement, in which everyone has a voice and knows they are valued
- Make culture change a vital and respected strategic objective.

A surprising turn of events

Franklin announced the results of the Culture Committee's work as part of a town hall meeting. The committee members were confident that the new vision for the culture would be well received. But surprisingly, as Franklin read the vision out loud, no one reacted. It fell flat. After covering the other items on the agenda, Franklin called the Culture Committee members into the conference room.

The members were dismayed. As they faced the outcomes together, Franklin remembered a similar experience. He shared this experience with the Culture Committee members: *"A few years ago, I was brought in as a division president along with other presidents to change the vision for our parent company's culture. As a group we argued, pushed back, and took the vision apart until it made sense to us. The result of our process in grappling with our thoughts and concerns was surprising. All of our hard conversations led to embracing and keeping the vision just as it was. I learned that the important part of what we'd done was the result of the honest dialogue and difficult conversations and moments we'd gone through together. My experience tells me we need to do something along these lines. If we create an opportunity for our employees to challenge this vision and allow them to have a say in defining what a successful culture should be, it just might enable us to develop a vision that speaks to everyone."*

OK, Now What?

To execute the idea of getting all employees engaged and having a voice in designing the new company culture, Franklin started with 80 participants for a three-day meeting. They were scheduled in maximally mixed groups (by division, race, gender, and level). Franklin introduced the program by establishing psychological safety. He said, *"No one will suffer for anything you say. You can speak your perspective, your truth, and I will have your back. I will protect you no matter what. If after this meeting there is anything that feels like a backlash, I will take care of it. I will not tolerate any back-stabbing as a result of what happens here."*

For the first exercise, participants, including members of the management board, met in groups of 15 to practice role-playing communication skills. These skills were based on the values they had worked to identify, including skills for giving and receiving feedback and dealing constructively with disagreement.

As the work began, the first task was for groups to identify the gaps between the current culture and the culture-vision statement. The next task was to process the feedback from each group. One of the important takeaways from the feedback was that leaders tended to tell people what to do, rather than listen to the suggestions and ideas of others.

In a room where everyone was present, a representative from each group and the management board members sat together in a circle in the middle of the room. As each representative shared the feedback from their group, the leaders worked to listen and ask clarifying questions. Their mission was to use their ability to *manage* their *reactions*—to listen without explaining, defending, or collecting "misinformation."

Afterwards, upon reflection with the management board members, Franklin said, *"I can't stress enough how hard it is to hang out there in listening mode. I know how difficult this was. You've earned your credibility through really hearing what needed to be said."*

As the process continued, there was a moment when an employee courageously shared a painful experience that occurred on the job. Everyone in the room felt the emotional impact of what had happened to her. Franklin, closely listening, was visibly moved. People noticed, and it demonstrated his empathy, making it safe for others to feel their emotions, too.

> Emotions aren't noise or a nuisance. They're data. The emotions people feel are a signal of whether a culture is toxic or healthy. The emotions people accept and reject are a window into what's valued in a culture.
>
> Sigal Barsade

Facilitators carefully captured the topics important to the culture change process. Then the participants formed action teams to address each topic and contributed recommendations to the management board regarding actions and solutions. Responding to these recommendations, the members of the management board listened and paraphrased. They continued to practice listening without explaining, justifying, or deciding anything—yet.

After the meeting ended, the action teams remained an active part of the culture change process, which served to provide continued employee involvement. In addition, Franklin encouraged the management board in their important role in leading the culture change. Embracing the challenge, the members of the management board integrated the new values-based behaviors into their interactions with employees. In doing so, over time they made a constructive difference in shifting the culture.

Recognizing and appreciating the hard work that

had been done, Franklin took the next step. He held a two-day strategic planning meeting with the Culture Committee. Everything that had been learned and understood during the three-day meeting became the basis for revising the vision-culture statement. Just as Franklin had predicted, the final version of the vision varied very little from the original one. The difference was that everyone's voice had been heard.

Franklin presented the vision, values, new norms, and behaviors at the town hall. He received a standing ovation. In the case of Pharma Bio Technologies, Franklin's intuition played out. Employee perspectives shifted to owning the vision statement once they were fully involved. Franklin said, *"Building the kind of culture we wanted for our company...examining, challenging, and defining the 'unwritten rules' of the culture, provided me and other leaders an opportunity to learn so much. What we learned contributed to bringing about a work environment where everyone now feels their part in the success of our business."*

"As a leader, it should be a priority to ensure employees understand the bigger picture and what purpose they fulfill. With a feeling of purpose, employees in an organization can accomplish great things for the long haul" (Kouzes and Posner, *The*

Leadership Challenge, 2007).

As Kouzes and Posner point out, people will keep going during challenging times when they believe in what they are doing. Why go through this time-consuming and challenging process? Creating a culture where everyone can contribute their best is an investment in a company's long-term success.

When people feel good about where they work, there is a freedom to perform at their best. Here is an example of how Franklin helped employees continue to develop a sense of pride in the company. At every town hall meeting he led, he invited a presenter—a patient, doctor, or customer—to tell their story about the impact of the company's work. Recognizing the need to acknowledge the work of the employees and the importance of creating a sustained sense of community, he was able to inspire everyone by pointing out that their efforts were integral to the end result. Those whose roles didn't come into direct contact with the customers could see and feel the meaningful impact of their work.

Franklin brought his *relationship intelligence* and heart to create BETA conditions and transform what wasn't working in his organization. With his combined *grit, grace* and *gravitas*, he successfully brought people to a place where they shared a sense of *Belonging* to something meaningful and where they could authentically feel *Empowered* in contributing to the mission. He created the conditions in which people felt *Trust* in him and each other and a sense of *Alignment* in what they were accomplishing together.

> Our lives are defined by our experiences, both at work and at home. And companies that recognize this and support their employees in these moments that matter will gain loyalty, boost retention, increase productivity and creativity and win the future.
>
> Arianna Huffington

Our next leader, Monica, received a promotion to executive vice president of the department of quality control and became a member of the senior leadership team. She inherited a department whose culture was in a crisis. The quality department's job was to perform lab research in order to get in front of and prevent errors from occurring. However, the operations department's employees, rather than holding themselves accountable for their mistakes, blamed the quality group's employees for not catching them. As a result of these dynamics, over time the quality department's employees became defensive and their morale fell to an all-time low.

Supervisors and their employees in that department felt unfairly blamed for accountabilities that were not theirs alone. Let's look at how Monica led the way to a resolution of this dysfunction in the culture.

> "Leadership affects the confidence of the staff and whether they see mistakes as opportunities for learning or failures that damage the self-worth of the employees. Leadership cultivates the foundation of culture to empower employees to achieve the company mission and realize how vital each of their contributions is to furthering those goals."
> William Craig

Monica stepped back to understand what could be causing the dysfunctions in the organization. She considered all the departments involved in the product development process and the more extensive cross-departmental interfaces. Monica recognized that the quality group could be working further upstream in partnership with product development to prevent downstream errors. She realized that reorganizing the process could potentially resolve the problems between the operations and quality departments.

Monica met with each department leader to discuss what she had observed and initiated a dialogue for resolution. She listened generously, partnering with other members on the senior leadership team. They came to a shared understanding of the current issues and how to resolve them. They decided to restructure the interfaces with product development and quality to ensure greater improvements in delivering their products to the market.

Monica's leadership brought about a breakthrough in which each department's employees took full accountability for quality. With BETA in mind, Monica set the conditions that would meet the needs of the quality department's employees. Her constructive approaches, behaviors, quality of her connection with people, and demeanor resulted in her being able to turn around negative attitudes and elevate the department's performance. As a result of the changes, the quality department's engagement survey score went from the lowest to the highest in the company. Monica's direct reports embraced her leadership, producing a cascading effect on others below them.

Monica's *grit* and *gravitas* provided even greater value through how she listened to understand and how she contributed her perspectives and ideas. Drawing on the *constructive power of grace*, Monica succeeded in strengthening a sense of connection and synergy among all involved.

Monica and Franklin both took the opportunity to lead people through a culture change—Monica grappled with a department in crisis, and Franklin grappled with the need for a new vision that could bring everyone together in his company. They each used the *constructive power of grace* to shift and elevate their people, processes, and performance.

"For better and worse, culture and leadership are inextricably linked. Founders and influential leaders often set new cultures in motion and imprint values and assumptions that persist for decades. Over time an organization's leaders can also shape culture through both conscious and unconscious actions." (*Harvard Business Review*, January-February 2018, "The Culture Factor")

For their efforts, Monica and Franklin became leaders even more worth following. Their reputations developed through their grasp of social needs, their empathetic understanding, and their application of *constructive power*. They strengthened their reputations through their approaches; their values became evident in their behavior, how they connected with people, and their caring and warmth. Drawing on the science of why and how the social brain is wired to connect, they succeeded in setting conditions to ensure sustained *Belonging, Trust, Empowerment,* and *Alignment* for and with their people.

In our next chapter, we delve into an aspect of our framework that is inseparable from *grace*, an element that is at the heart of exemplary, transformational leadership.

Chapter 8
Grace and Generosity

In this chapter, we will look at leaders who led with the constructive power of grace and see what they have been able to accomplish as a result. You will see how their approaches, their behaviors, the quality of how they connected with people, and the presence of grace in their demeanors were beneficial for those they led and brought value to their organizations. We'll begin to explore the element of generosity. We'll examine why and how it is an important aspect of leadership that is integrated with the constructive power of grace.

Our experiences have led us to understand that generosity is at the heart of the *constructive power of grace.* It is inseparable from the word *grace* because every time you are able to choose your *constructive power,* every time you work to overcome your reactions, restore your presence of mind, and go beyond emotionally charged ways of responding to people, your generosity is involved. It takes generosity on the part of a leader to make the choice to lead with *constructive power.* It is much easier to lash out, criticize, withhold support when you don't like something someone did, or hold what they did against them.

What are some characteristics that describe leaders you see as generous? Generous leaders make themselves available. They bring compassion and openheartedness to their work with people. For example, seeking to understand is generous vs. assuming you already know what someone means or is about to say. Listening with the intent to understand is generous vs. just waiting to say what you want. It is generous to give full attention to someone. In a social context generosity is a part of *relationship intelligence.* It involves skills and competences to facilitate interactions with others, for example, interpersonal skills and facilitating a discussion with members of your team to resolve differences and restore alignment.

Generosity is the quality of being kind and caring. Consider the difference in leaders who lack generosity: If you unpack what is going on in the *reactive zone,* ego, power struggles, and right and wrong filtering that brings judgmental accusations to bear on others, you'll notice many opportunities to block mutual understanding and acceptance.

> "Any fool can criticize, complain and condemn—and most fools do. But it takes character and self-control to be understanding and forgiving."
> Dale Carnegie

The absence of *grace* in a leader is the absence of a kind of generosity toward people. Generosity is the ability to get beyond and see beyond blame, shame, and guilt to address problems and issues constructively. It is generous to look more deeply, to get beyond an all-too-common reaction that you are right and someone else is wrong, to know your influence matters and to be aware of the different outcomes that occur as a result of choosing positive rather than negative approaches.

When a leader lacks generosity

One evening, we met with a client who demonstrated some of the imbalances that occur with *grit* and *gravitas* when a spirit of generosity—a hallmark of exemplary leaders—is missing in a leader's presence and impact. The client, talking about strengths she'd identified in herself, contrasted what she saw as her strengths with weaknesses she found in others. She spoke about attitudes she saw in other women in her organization when they came to meetings with upper management. She said they sounded as if they lacked confidence or did not know what they were talking about. *"They lack gravitas,"* she said. The judgmental tone with which she described these other women revealed that she was not inclined to offer guidance to help them develop. Even as she made insightful and important observations, her leadership, in terms of supporting and empowering others to develop strengths she knew were critical, stopped there. It went no further than her criticism of what she saw as their faults.

We were able to observe in this client the impact of her leadership and her presence. Her approach to leading meetings was described in interviews with her team: *"She pontificates, she comes across as pompous, officious, and condescending."* Would she have been surprised to learn that others would have given anything to avoid having to deal with her? Yes, she had *gravitas* and she also had *grit*. She had a wealth of experience and could have tough conversations; she was thorough and tenacious. But she acted in an arrogant and condescending manner; the light that went on for us in that meeting crystalized something essential missing in her leadership—the absence of *grace*. She had the potential to be an extraordinary leader, but rather than share her knowledge and support generously and empower the women with whom she found fault, she withheld her support from them.

What could this client have accomplished as a leader had the *grit* and *gravitas* she possessed been infused with the *constructive power of grace*? What of value is lost when the spirit of generosity is not present in a leader? When a leader supports and empowers those they lead, a different order of results becomes possible. Why? Because these leaders know how to bring out the best in those they lead and create a space in which people can excel.

When generosity is present in a leader

In the example that follows, a leader handling an unexpected situation successfully intervenes through the *constructive power of grace*. What occurs exemplifies the spirit of generosity in action.

Sitting around a conference table, Bill, the COO of a large global organization, began to pointedly criticize Stephanie, a young manager who reported to the SVP Anika. As Bill's angry comments flew across the table, Stephanie, feeling conspicuously criticized in front of everyone at the table, began to shrink back in shame and embarrassment. Anika leaned forward, her posture almost shielding

Stephanie, and calmly addressed Bill by outlining the background information and the logic and reason for what Stephanie had shared. Anika's approach created an immediate shift in the tension in the room, which served to neutralize the negativity coming across the table and allowed a productive conversation to follow. The tenor of the conversation shifted away from criticism and blame as Anika skillfully intervened, creating the conditions for the issues at hand to be constructively resolved.

Following the meeting, Stephanie let Anika know how much she appreciated her support. Other attendees let Anika know they'd never seen anything like that, with questions and statements such as, *"How did you do that?"* and *"That was amazing!"* Generously, she gave Bill the benefit of the doubt, knowing he was mainly a very fair and even-tempered person and that he must for some reason, be having a bad day. She had the presence of mind to take a constructive approach and avoided calling him out in front of everyone when she intervened on Stephanie's behalf. She acted in a way that created psychological safety for Stephanie and everyone else at the table.

What made Anika so successful? What skills are involved in being able to diffuse a reactive situation in the way that Anika did? Using *reaction management* and *relationship intelligence* skills, Anika drew on her *constructive power.* Her direct and nonjudgmental approach, her calming behavior, and the quality of how she connected with the COO inspired everyone at the table. Her demeanor modeled a generous and constructive way of dealing with negativity and resulted in elevating the emotional state from a negative to a positive one. In the moment Anika leaned forward, she used her energy to neutralize the negativity rather than resist what was occurring. She took the moment in hand, intervened with the *constructive power of grace*, and created a transformative impact.

What is the value of using one's generosity in being able to look beyond reactions to a negative situation and to forego opinions that would be easy to form about someone?

It would have been easy to consider the COO in a very negative light. But Anika's generous approach took into consideration that Bill might be having a rough day. She saw what had occurred as something out of character rather than a pattern of his behavior. Rather than criticizing him in public and instead, giving him the benefit of the doubt, she recognized that almost anyone can become reactive at times. Stephanie was able to recover quickly with Anika's intervention on her behalf. Anika's approach of putting *grace's* spirit of generosity into action led to Bill becoming more self-aware. He took it upon himself to apologize to Stephanie in private.

Let's take a moment to consider what occurred in terms of how Anika integrated the *constructive power of grace* and how it flowed generously through her approaches, her behaviors, the quality of her connection with those involved, and her demeanor.

What can you see in the **approaches** she took?

- In her approach Anika responded in a graceful way by intervening constructively on behalf of Stephanie, Bill, and everyone who was around the table.

- Her approach was to intervene, to lead with compassion in a nonjudgmental way. Her *relationship intelligence* enabled her to see behind Bill's behavior in a moment when he didn't manage his reaction well.

What can you see in her **behaviors**?

- Anika spoke in a way that brought context and clarification to the issues under consideration.

- She leaned forward protectively and spoke in a

way that shifted the conversation to a more constructive dialogue.

- She elevated the emotional state from negative to positive.

What was the quality of her **connection** with the people involved?

- Anika connected with those involved in ways that were constructive, protective, safe, knowledgeable, and respectful.
- Her connection with Bill was respectful, professional, and compassionate. She was generous in giving him the benefit of the doubt.

What was evident in her **demeanor**?

- Anika's demeanor was grounded and caring; she was a safe harbor in the incident.
- She was open and nonjudgmental, calmly confronting the issue at hand.
- In handling the situation, her *grit* and *gravitas* were infused with the *constructive power of grace.*

Anika used the *constructive power of grace* to

take control of a sudden reactive situation. Our next example is about a leader who used the *constructive power of grace* to confront a reactive situation that was brought to her attention, one where anger and animosity between two employees had been festering for a long time.

The power of generosity in the midst of crisis

Michele was the COO of a group of medical offices. She highly valued the physicians and staff who worked in each of the offices she oversaw. She was dedicated to ensuring that physicians and employees were empowered in their mission to provide the highest level of care to the patients they served. Each office was run by a physician leader, and although the culture of each office differed as a result, every employee shared an understanding of what was expected of them in terms of their individual performance as well as the overall performance of each office. Michele's commitment and dedication as a leader were evident in the constructive approaches she took, the respect and transparency of her behaviors and the caring, empowering ways she connected with people, as well as the calm objectivity that came across in her demeanor.

As in many organizations, there are times when staff members don't get along, when tempers flare, when there are instances of people not pulling their weight—for example, coming in late, leaving early. And there are also times when more serious situations arise. Michele's direct reports took care of many of these problems. Still, they also knew they could count on her to provide wise counsel when they brought more difficult situations to her attention.

One of her direct reports came to her with an escalating situation occurring between two doctors that had reached a crisis point. Recognizing costs to both doctors in their practice, their staff, and their overall group if the situation was allowed to continue, Michele asked for our help in facilitating a resolution.

The process started by meeting with each doctor individually. To establish trust and psychological safety, Michele assured each of them that they had her full support and commitment. She told them she would assist them in finding a way to resolve their differences—acknowledging that this might not seem possible to them at the moment. In these preliminary, confidential sessions, they each shared their perspective of why circumstances were the way they were and the reasons they found themselves in this highly charged, unworkable situation with one another.

Dr. Robinson was the physician leader of this particular office, responsible for overseeing the quality of patient care. He was someone with a great deal of intelligence, expertise, and a commitment to patients. He had a desire for his staff to feel they were a part of something meaningful where each of their roles mattered. Yet here he was, dealing with the lack of cooperation and alignment from a member of his team that had become an insurmountable obstacle. He knew something needed to be done to face and deal with the situation.

One of the main problems Dr. Robinson described to us was a lack of respect he felt from Dr. Miller regarding his responsibilities ensuring the quality of patient care. In far too many interactions with Dr. Miller, he'd not only felt a lack of respect from her, he found her to be uncooperative, resistant, and inconsiderate. Dr. Robinson shared that he'd never had this kind of situation before, and it had become intolerable for him to work with her. He was very concerned about the staff in the office he oversaw. The staff members had taken sides and split into two camps, which made the workplace much more difficult. His attempts to talk with Dr. Miller and to reason with her had led nowhere, and he now knew without a doubt that working with her was no longer possible.

Dr. Miller shared that she felt threatened by actions Dr. Robinson took to ensure the quality of service that had to do with her work. She saw his actions as a lack of respect for her work. She felt that she had worked hard to establish herself and build her patient practice. She resisted what she saw as his attempts *"to control"* her.

Work in an organization is a social phenomenon, a place where there are social contracts around the interfacing of roles and responsibilities. People are accountable to the person they report to; in this case, Dr. Miller reported to Dr. Robinson. The social contract was that he was to oversee the quality of all work performed in that office—including hers.

Dr. Miller shared that she didn't understand why he needed to go over her cases with her when she was "a good physician" who knew what she was doing. She resented him asking about her work. Dr. Miller had taken great offense the prior week when, as she was finishing up a procedure with a client, he'd come into the room to see how things had gone. Afterwards she was so enraged at him for having done this. The annoyance and animosity she felt toward him had escalated into another heated argument.

Part of psychological safety is having the chance to express thoughts and feelings that are difficult to say. The next part of the process was organized for the purpose of facilitating a resolution through direct communication between Dr. Miller and Dr. Robinson. Sitting around the table together, Michele reminded them of the importance of taking this opportunity to communicate openly with one another. She stressed the importance of finding a resolution, noting that this situation was costly to each of them personally as well as to the organization. She told them she was counting on them to have an honest discussion about what led up to this situation in the hopes that a resolution to the problem could be found. If not, she would find herself in a situation where she would feel forced to make a decision she would rather not have to make.

In a process such as this one sometimes the road to resolution is a difficult one. Why? Because interpersonal dynamics can escalate before they can authentically be resolved; it is almost as if escalation is a step in getting there. It is also important to remember that in a conflict such as this when the amygdala goes into fight or flight mode, higher order thinking shuts down, compromising the ability to solve problems and making it more difficult to communicate constructively. There, in the *reactive zone,* the sense of connection between people is temporarily disabled. Accusations and defensiveness about who is right and who is wrong get in the way of seeing someone as a human being rather than as "the enemy" and get in the way of seeing through the lens of understanding and compassion. It can be difficult to become aware of another's struggle, another's vulnerability, another's pain. Both Dr. Robinson and Dr. Miller were feeling threatened, and their reactions flew across the table at the enemy they saw sitting across from them—each other. Then came the moment in the process when it looked as though a resolution would be impossible to achieve. Dr. Robinson got up from the table and walked out of the room saying, *"I can't see this working out, and I don't want to work with you any longer."* His words were blunt and direct. Door closed. Game over.

Dr. Robinson's words hung in the air with finality. Stunned, Dr. Miller realized that her worst fears might have just been confirmed. She struggled to find her footing as worried thoughts and emotions swirled around in her mind, the difficulties she would have to face of relocating, of rebuilding her practice, of having to change her daughter's school, and of losing the friends she'd made.

Without the presence of understanding and compassion, when reactions reach this kind of impasse a resolution can seem unachievable. Would it surprise you to know that the relationship between them improved and resolved from there? It takes a willingness and a generosity on one's part to find a way, especially because compassion, while part of what it is to be human, can become blunted by anger and misunderstanding. When we begin to understand each other, our compassion can emerge without effort. Human understanding is a doorway to compassion.

Grace has many faces but the feeling is unmistakable

Dr. Robinson asked to speak to us privately. Michele, committed to facilitating the resolution, joined the conversation. She shared a personal story of her own about how she once found herself in a stressful, competitive situation with a colleague. She decided to have a conversation with this colleague. She addressed their competitive dynamics and suggested that if they worked together, instead of against each other, they could form an alliance that would make them exceedingly successful as a team. Her colleague took her up on her suggestion and everything changed—for the better. From that moment on their relationship became a *"powerhouse that distinguished them both."*

After sharing this story with Dr. Robinson, Michele said, *"I understand if you don't want to continue. I will respect your decision either way but, as a leader, isn't it valuable to be able to deal effectively with people who are being difficult?"*

Dr. Robinson thought long and hard about what he should do, prompted by the following questions: *"What if this was an opportunity for your development as a leader? What if you found a way to transcend all of the acrimony in the situation to not only heal your relationship with Dr. Miller, but also resolve the rift that has affected everyone in your office and caused people to take sides? Can you consider what might be underneath Dr. Miller's reactions and behaviors? Would you be surprised to learn that although you see her as competent, she doesn't realize that? That she thinks you are questioning her work because you don't think she's doing a good job? She wants to be recognized for being good at what she does."*

We then shared some of the other comments Dr. Miller had taken the risk of expressing when Dr. Robinson had angrily left the room. He became aware of challenges Dr. Miller was dealing with as a single parent and how hard it had been for her to establish her roots here. He began to understand what it must feel like for her and how hard it would be, given his refusal to work with her any longer, for her to have to leave and start all over again.

In that moment, Dr. Robinson saw Dr. Miller as a human being with personal vulnerabilities, challenges, and professional aspirations she'd worked hard to achieve. Through this lens he was able to understand her fears and concerns. His compassion emerged as he began to understand how she had been struggling. Compassion and understanding are connected. Compassion opens the door to understanding (for example, *I don't just hear you, I understand what it has been like for you*) and understanding opens the door to compassion (for example, *I can feel the discomfort, stress or pain you've been going through.*)

Dr. Robinson decided to take the opportunity Michele had suggested—to evolve as a leader. He found himself saying, *"I want to hit the reset button and go on in a better way."*

Dr. Robinson returned to the conference room where Dr. Miller was waiting. As the two made eye contact, immediately she could see and feel the shift in his expression and his demeanor; the anger was gone. He put out his hand to Dr. Miller and said, *"Let's hit the reset button and go on in a better way together. I really respect you. I think you are an extremely competent physician. You've come such a long way. My responsibility for quality and operations in our office in no way is meant to make you feel that I don't value and respect you. I'm not trying to check up on you because I don't think you are competent, but I can see that it could feel that way to you. You are extremely competent. I'm just trying to do what I've been asked to do."*

In addition, he said, *"What if we thought about a goal we could have where we collaborate regarding the quality of service to our clients? We could get together on a regular basis and identify our most effective approaches and outcomes. We could generate a compendium of our best practices and even share them with others in our group. How does this sound to you?"*

She expressed her appreciation for the opportunity to go on in a better way. She was surprised and relieved, not having expected the situation to work out. She felt a genuine sense of connection and alignment and was grateful for a positive way to go forward together. Dr. Miller also expressed the respect she had for Dr. Robinson's experience and expertise. She let him know she valued his knowledge and felt she could learn a great deal from him.

In this example, the drama of the situation had escalated to an unworkable point and yet, after several difficult conversations, moments of *grace*, compassion, and understanding had emerged. No one was more surprised than they were. Part of the spirit of generosity involves the desire to reawaken our compassion when it shuts down.

Healing the divide

Up to this point the office staff were used to seeing Dr. Robinson and Dr. Miller at odds with one another. As a critical part of hitting the reset button, they gathered their staff together the next day. Together, both doctors shared that they had resolved their differences and acknowledged how difficult things had been. The staff was relieved and felt reassured that the animosity between them had been resolved. Together, they worked on how they would all go forward in a better way. Dr. Robinson and Dr. Miller led the way to establishing and sustaining a reset of their culture.

Michele could have taken a very different approach in handling this critical situation. Given her commitment to the people she leads and her dedication to ensuring that employees are empowered in their mission to provide the highest level of care, she chose to invest her time and resources and have professional guidance to generate a breakthrough if possible. She knew she was taking a risk, but the upside was significant. If it worked out, she would be able to salvage the fine talent she already had in place, elevate their emotional state from a negative to a positive one, and help them find a way to restore a sense of *Belonging, Empowerment, Trust,* and *Alignment*—all of which represented a win for everyone.

Let's review what occurred in terms of how Dr. Robinson and Dr. Miller finally found the compassion and understanding they needed to be able to integrate the *constructive power of grace* into their *grit* and *gravitas*.

What shifted in their approaches toward one another?

- Dr. Robinson and Dr. Miller approached a process they were dreading and took the risk of experiencing the process together, facing the difficult conversations they needed to have.

- Their approach toward each other elevated from a dynamic that was contentious, reactive, and negative to one that became understanding, compassionate, and cooperative.

What shifted in their behavior?

- Dr. Robinson and Dr. Miller's behavior shifted away from being focused on their reactions to finding their way to better understanding themselves and each other.

- Their behavior shifted from resistance, anger, and contentiousness to kindness, consideration, and respect for each other.

- They aligned on and executed a plan to address the divisiveness in their culture and shift the dynamics from divided to united.

What shifted in the quality of their connection with one another?

- Dr. Robinson and Dr. Miller dissolved the animosity they felt toward each other.

- They shifted from feeling like enemies to restoring their respectful cooperation and connection as colleagues.

- They felt mutually connected to creating a future that mattered.

What shifted in their demeanor toward each other and their organization?

- Dr. Robinson and Dr. Miller's demeanor reflected the change in they had both worked to achieve. Whereas before their demeanor projected the agitation, annoyance, and resentment they felt for one another, now their demeanor reflected a collegial respect, warmth, and alignment.

- Their staff saw the change in the demeanor of both doctors; they noticed that the animosity they had come to expect was gone, changing the atmosphere of the office for the better.

Let's consider generosity. Was it generous of Dr. Robinson to reconsider his reactions to what he saw as Dr. Miller's lack of cooperation? Was it generous to take some responsibility and to choose to evolve as a leader, rather than walk away from the situation? Was it generous of him to consider Dr. Miller's concerns? Why does generosity matter? When you care enough to be willing, your willingness to understand another's experience is generous. It helps you awaken your compassion. Compassion changes your emotional state toward someone, replacing the lack of awareness and hardheadedness that come from the imbalances of *grit* and *gravitas* with the mindful openheartedness of *grace*. What difference can you see this having in the dynamics between people on teams and in the cultures of organizations?

Generosity and the constructive power of *grace*

If we look at the leaders we've met in this chapter, Anika chose to act and listen constructively in a way that turned a contentious, negative situation into a calm and constructive one. Dr. Miller and Dr. Robinson got past their seemingly unresolvable differences to finally listen to one another beyond the reactions that had been getting in their way.

There is always the choice to be made as to how to deal with challenges that arise. Every time we turn to the *constructive power of grace* to address difficulties, breakdowns, and challenges, the spirit of generosity is active. It brings about important outcomes and benefits such as the way leaders are able to elevate people's emotional state from negative to positive and to increase participation and engagement. As we said in the beginning of this chapter, generosity is at the heart of the *constructive power of grace*. It is inseparable from the word *grace* because every time you choose constructive power over reactive, emotionally charged ways of responding to people, your generosity will be making an important difference.

It takes generosity for people to get past these kinds of moments—generosity for oneself and for the other people involved in the reaction. It takes commitment to be aware in the moment of a reaction and to discipline yourself to mentally pause and step outside of it. When a reaction takes over, it can be difficult to "break the spell." It isn't always easy to find the pause button Viktor Frankl describes and to recover ourselves. Some reactions are easier than others to "shake off." But until you break "the spell" of a reaction—help yourself transcend the fight or flight instinct and find the pause button—your stress response will extract a physical and emotional toll. In the midst of reactions, people—yourself and others—feel emotional pain. Who wouldn't welcome a lifeline of compassion and understanding, an olive branch of forgiveness, or jump at the chance to go on in a better way?

Chapter 9
Using *Grit, Grace and Gravitas* to Prevail in Adversity

Earlier in this book we cited Dr. Gavin Dagley's research that included feedback relating to what he called a "dark presence," which describes a leader with a presence that is negative, intimidating, and unsupportive. In this chapter, as we promised earlier, we look at a client's challenge in dealing with a leader's dark presence. We will examine how one can address imbalances in grit and gravitas, turn to the constructive power of grace to survive, and ultimately thrive in a difficult work situation with a colleague.

Many of our clients have found themselves challenged because of power struggles and inequities due to working in an adverse, political environment where destructive behavior is tolerated. More than a few of the situations these clients faced involved a boss, direct report, or colleague whose goal was to undermine others. They draw attention to themselves in order to elevate their self-importance at the *expense* of others. Their negative approaches and behaviors, the intimidating ways they connect with people, and the arrogance present in their demeanor ensured they were the dominant power player in their organization. Let's consider this, along with Dr. Dagley's research, where respondents defined a *negative* or *dark presence* as follows:

Negative interpersonal behavior patterns and values-in-action included: "behaviours in four areas: **aggression** (that such people were 'critical,' 'intimidating,' 'judgmental,' 'condescending,' 'demeaning,' 'bullying,' 'hostile,' and 'overbearing'); **aloofness** (the person's behaviours were 'cold,' 'dismissive,' and 'remote'); **political behaviour** (the person was 'manipulative,' and good at 'managing upwards'); and finally, **unpredictability** (including '[you] never knew where you stood,' a lack of openness, and the person 'kept everyone on edge'). Values-in-action responses included comments about arrogance, dishonesty, intolerance, the primacy of personal agendas, and distrustfulness of others" (Dagley, 2013, p. 10).

In the research, interpersonal behavior patterns and values-in-action overlapped with power use. The most frequent comment regarding power use was about when leaders "...'[made] people feel inadequate—fearful,' and '[used] fear through threat and humiliation.' Other comments (from respondents) included: the use of 'micro-management,' the leader 'damaging reputations through [publicly] coaching [subordinate managers],' and that 'no disagreement [was] allowed'" (Dagley, 2013, p. 10).

Our client, Irene, was dealing with a situation that relates to the elements Dagley describes as a *negative* or *dark presence*. You will see how Irene came to terms with the realities of dealing with a colleague's *dark presence* and how she prevailed to successfully take charge of her leadership, her executive presence, and her impact.

Irene is a remarkably dedicated and accomplished professional in a financial services firm. Year after year she succeeded in surpassing the results of the previous year. We will look at how she was able to accomplish this while having to contend with a colleague, Brad, who sought to undermine her efforts.

How Irene's situation became intolerable

Irene and Brad were peers who were on equal footing as partners in their last company before merging with another financial services firm.

Although Brad and Irene both had partner status in the new entity, Irene noticed that Brad was aggressively seeking advancement for himself. When the larger client opportunities came about, he made sure they were given to him. Concurrently, the incidences of Brad treating Irene with disrespect increased, as did occurrences of discrediting her behind her back.

Irene was informed by her current boss that the company was reorganizing and she would now be reporting to Brad. She asked if there was a way to continue to report to her current boss but was told that with the reorganization that wouldn't be possible. Irene had a great deal of concern and trepidation as the transition took place. In terms of who she was to report to, there was no other option at the moment.

Irene knew, without a doubt, that this change was not in her best interest. Her concerns were confirmed almost immediately. Brad's negative attitude toward her became increasingly problematic. He continued to withhold client opportunities from her. He wrested accounts out from under her that she had secured for the firm, and he found ways of taking credit for results she'd been instrumental in delivering.

Brad's negativity toward Irene came to her attention in other ways. Colleagues let her know of demeaning remarks made behind her back. Whenever Irene presented to their group, Brad's disinterest in what she was presenting would be expressed by his working on his phone or by his leaving the room and not returning. Whatever his motivation—ego? control issues? competitive power plays?—his behavior toward her stemmed from some need on his part to diminish her directly, as well as in the eyes of others, and to prevent her from gaining status and recognition. Brad's actions are examples of a leader's *negative* or *dark presence*.

Gossip aimed at having someone be less well thought of is a damaging ploy with lasting effects. Irene spent the majority of her time on the road serving clients, but there were also times she worked from the home office. Because Brad had gossiped about her and discredited her behind her back, Irene felt ill at ease working in their home office when Brad was there.

Before we look at how Irene handled this challenging situation with Brad, you are probably wondering why she didn't just leave the firm. Here are some of the reasons. Irene cared about the client relationships she had built up over the years, people who she was dedicated to, people who valued her support and guidance. She didn't want to lose them.

She had earned the trust and respect of these clients, which meant a great deal to Irene. She also didn't want to lose newer clients she was in the midst of advising. There was also a very restrictive non-compete agreement to take into consideration. After decades of hard work, she did not relish the idea of what she would have to forego to start all over again.

How Irene successfully organized her efforts to deal with her situation

On several occasions, Irene tried to have a conversation with Brad to neutralize the negativity she felt and improve their dynamics. Her efforts were unsuccessful. Communication to resolve unworkable dynamics can produce miracles, but that only happens when all parties involved share a sincere commitment to resolve issues. Irene realized that working things out with Brad was not something she could achieve. How could Irene mitigate the negative impact of Brad's disrespectful and judgmental behavior, including the damage he'd done gossiping about her behind the scenes? In our conversations she shared that this negativity had affected her self-confidence. She decided to concentrate her efforts in a different direction, one that would help her lift her emotional state to a more positive one and help build her confidence from within.

Irene focused on increasing her well-being, as well as strengthening her core sense of respect and regard for the consummate professional she is. She became more and more present to the value she added and her contributions to the growth of the firm. Irene set personal boundaries, shifting her habit of needing validation from Brad and not allowing the inequities she'd been up against to harden her heart. She put together a chronology of the negative actions and injustices that had occurred, updating it as any further situations took place. Having this record at her disposal served as an important resource. It shifted her perspective from feeling victimized by the situation to feeling confident that she could handle this in a powerful way at the right time. She would be ready to stand up for herself when the opportunity presented itself.

The objective viewpoint she secured for herself gave her the distance she needed from taking Brad's behavior personally. She was able to see Brad as someone operating with a very different set of values and ethics. At that time she needed to do some work to build her confidence in her considerable knowledge and experience.

Irene worked on clarifying her internal bearings. She identified what she held most dear in being a trusted advisor, which included her aspirations for making a difference in meeting her clients' needs and contributing at a high level to her organization's success.

Together, we looked at the question of what was the driving force within her. Why did she care so much about people? Such questions led Irene to identify a legacy of service and trust she had observed in her dad. Her father had served as a great inspiration to her, and she realized how much of his influence was present in how she led and related to people. She recalled how she'd seen her father in his relationships with his clients. She saw how they relied on him and how safe they felt with him. She saw how his kindness and compassion provided a safe harbor in dealing with the problems they were struggling to resolve.

Irene identified what mattered to her in relationships, including team members she worked most closely with, and how important it was to make sure they felt appreciated for their efforts. For example, if she received a call from a client—which frequently happened—to thank her for the work that had been done for them, she would reach out to members of the team. She would tell them about how happy the client was and make sure they felt appreciated for what they had contributed. Members of her team expressed their gratitude for her calls of appreciation. She also advocated for her staff, publicly acknowledging their talents and contributions. Irene realized that her desire to consistently give people the experience of being appreciated, considered, and cared for was another hallmark of her professionalism and leadership.

Irene came to recognize and appreciate that the *constructive power of grace* was a superpower that came naturally to her. The *grace* that flowed through her *grit* and her *gravitas* was observable in her approaches, her behaviors, the quality of how she connected with people, and her demeanor. This was evident to the clients she served, the men and women she worked with in her industry, the people who attended her presentations at conferences, and the high potential men and women she mentored. They all received the benefits of her considerable knowledge and her ability to get things to the finish line. They all valued the warmth and sincerity of her commitment to empower and appreciate people.

Along with clearly defining her leadership aspirations, Irene also examined the imbalances of her *grit* and *gravitas*. Concerning *gravitas,* she saw that she needed to increase her permission to own her power and influence. Regarding Dagley's *dark presence* and, specifically, Brad's unpredictability, Irene never knew when he would put her down publicly. She felt unsafe and judged by him, and she acknowledged the damage this had done to reduce her self-confidence. People with this imbalance in *gravitas* minimize their accomplishments, their growth, and their development. Their self-confidence suffers as a result.

Irene also saw how this imbalance in her *gravitas* connected with an imbalance in her *grit*.

Facing her imbalance of *grit*, she noticed her discomfort with power and the reluctance she'd had to own her power. She also faced the intimidation she'd felt as a result of how Brad used his power. She worked on this aspect of her imbalance. Women often need to modulate how they deal with power. It is all too easy for a woman to be branded as difficult. To avoid this label, women can be reluctant to push back in moments that matter, and they have difficulty in setting boundaries. How do you set boundaries, protect yourself, and apply what the *constructive power of grace* can offer you in these kinds of situations? A first question to answer is: What is in my control and what isn't?

Irene was in control of raising her *grit* by constructively managing her reactions and her willingness to own her power and her *gravitas* by no longer allowing herself to be thrown off center. She paid attention to her tendency to feel diminished, slighted, or hurt by some action Brad had taken, such as efforts to undermine her by excluding her from meetings and withholding information she should have had as a partner. Irene trained herself to turn to her internal bearings and keep her leadership aspirations present by reading them over daily. Using this practice over time, she experienced a breakthrough. She became stronger, more resilient, and more authentically confident about who she was. This was a turning point in her development as Irene took back her power. When triggered, Irene could now manage and mitigate the threat of Brad's negative behavior.

Not all situations like this have a happy ending. Irene's did. After a year there was another reorganization. A new global leader, whose vision and values were constructive and inspiring, took the helm. The door opened for Irene to report to someone new who has a great deal of respect for her. She now looks forward every day to working in this collaborative environment. She never takes for granted the mutual support and partnering that are the norm in this culture.

Chapter 10
Conclusion:
Grace is the game changer

We have seen time and again that what distinguishes great leaders is their capacity for *grace*. Their *grit* and their *gravitas*, infused with the skills and qualities of *grace*, bring exceptional value to those they lead. Why? Great leaders understand and embrace the responsibilities that go beyond their job descriptions. They welcome the opportunities to inspire and bring out the best in those they lead. They set out to generate a culture in which people thrive and where the men and women they lead have a sense of being a part of something meaningful and feel empowered, valued, and appreciated. Their *reaction management* and *relationship intelligence* skills are exemplary. They earn the trust, respect, and affection of those they lead because they understand, pay attention to and listen well to people, and treat people with respect. Great leaders develop teams of men and women who are in step with one another to accomplish the outcomes that matter. Together, they face the challenges that come with the hard times and share pride in the successes that are part of the good times.

Let's revisit Mary for a moment. As you may recall, Mary's boss had let her know, following a particularly challenging quarter, that her team was unhappy with her leadership. She'd asked him, *"What do you want: results or happy people?"* And he'd assured her that *"the best leaders achieve both."* Mary achieved results by relying on her *grit* and *gravitas* but getting her team to the finish line was obtained at their expense. She led the charge without the *constructive power of grace*. Her approaches, behaviors, quality of how she connected with members of her team, and her demeanor had a negative, depleting impact on those she led. To Mary's credit, this conversation with her boss became a turning point in both her mind and heart.

Today more and more leaders are increasing their self-awareness. They are choosing to address imbalances in their *grit* and *gravitas* and achieve the transformations their *constructive power* makes possible. Taking steps to define and develop their *highest leadership aspirations* is providing them with a sustained sense of purpose with which to shape their impact. These leaders are honing their ability to *elevate emotional states* and inspire those they lead through the tough times. As one client put it, they like themselves *"better this way."*

Presence, it turns out, is no mystery. It isn't a function of having charisma or a larger than life personality. It doesn't require you to be an extrovert. It is important to remember that you are the one who decides the quality, substance, and impact of your presence. The power is totally in your hands to decide which qualities and skills will help you evolve your leadership and your presence. A place to begin is to pay attention to the effect your presence is currently having on those you lead. Secondly, you can ask for feedback and objectively look at the imbalances that are brought to your attention. For instance, as one leader shared, *"I need to increase my reaction management and learn to pause and choose a constructive way to respond to situations that are hard for me to handle."* What will benefit you? Be honest with yourself. Start with one change you want to make. Believe it or not, small steps add up to big changes.

A leader's evolution doesn't happen all at once. In the process of your development, each of the efforts you make is important to the growth you are working to achieve. As you take risks and practice using the *constructive power of grace,* remember that the changes you make—no matter how small they may seem to you—will produce a momentum, a cumulative positive effect that will be beneficial for you and those you lead. Reminding ourselves of the guiding skills and qualities of *grace,* we become present to bringing out the best in people through considerate, thoughtful, and stabilizing means, even in the worst of circumstances. *Grace* is the presence in a leader of a caring, compassionate, generosity toward others.

> The challenge of a leader is to be strong but not rude; be kind but not weak; be bold but not a bully; be humble but not timid; be proud but not arrogant; have humor but without folly.
>
> Jim Rohn

You can use the guide provided in the Addendum, *Finding Your Internal Bearings Exercise,* which provides examples of what too much and too little *grit* and *gravitas* look, feel, and sound like. You can use this to understand the impact you are having. Take any situation and note what you see in your approaches, behaviors, the quality of your connection with people, and your demeanor. Notice the impact you have on others. *Are you aligned with your highest aspirations as a leader with the internal bearings you've defined? To what extent are you now able to integrate the skills and qualities of grace? What habits are you building?*

It takes courage to look at ourselves honestly. Given that none of us is perfect, we hope you've gained an objective, nonjudgmental lens and perspective to examine the specific imbalances you are identifying for yourself. The evolution that is occurring within you will become quite evident to you at some point. For example, you may find you have a greater sense of well-being or you may see positive feedback coming from your colleagues, family, and those you lead. As you notice the differences in how you are relating to others and handling upsets, along with increases in productivity and results, we hope you'll feel a renewed sense of fulfillment through your leadership. Let us know what you are finding and what successes and challenges you can now handle in ways that are surprising you.

Arianna Huffington wrote in her book, *The Fourth Instinct,* that Françoise Gilot once told her there were "doors in time." Arianna noted that "we are facing such a door in time—an opening for great possibilities of a new being, for a breakthrough in our evolution. For the first time something vast and epic as the destiny of mankind depends on something as personal and intimate as the way each one of us chooses to live, think, and behave."

What becomes possible when you lead, "live, think, and behave" through your constructive power? What becomes possible in your evolution as a leader? What can transform as a result of your *grit* and *gravitas* and having the *constructive power of grace* flowing through them? How can you lead the way forward through the "door in time" that is an opening for our evolution? As Abraham Lincoln said in his inaugural address, we need to turn now *"to the better angels of our nature."* They are there, waiting for us to call on them, waiting for us to lead from them. May the darkness move aside for you with respect for who you are.

Addendum
Finding Your Internal Bearings Exercise

Before you begin this exercise, take a moment to absorb this fact about your leadership. Your presence is unique, and the impact of your leadership and your presence is felt hundreds of times a day by those you live, lead and work with. What kind of impact are you having?

Remember that your presence is a major influence on whether those you lead are inspired, engaged, and empowered to produce the results that matter. Why? Because the impact of your presence is seen and felt through the approaches you take, your behavior, the quality of how you connect with people, and your demeanor. Defining and leading through your highest leadership aspirations are critical components of your ability to lead with the *constructive power of grace.*

Step 1: Defining my *internal bearings*—getting to the heart of the matter with the *constructive power of grace*.

Context: Your highest leadership aspirations are distinct from your personal goals. Take a moment to consider your ambitions alongside your highest leadership aspirations. There is a clear relationship between your "ambitions" and your "higher aspirations." Your ambitions will reflect your goals: what you are working to achieve for yourself. They relate to factors such as your status in the organization, which can include goals such as making partner or joining the executive team. Your ambitions also can include your financial goals and some combination of salary and bonus that lets you know you are hitting the mark of what you've set out to achieve. In this exercise you are looking for *your highest leadership aspirations*: your values—the things that are of the greatest importance to you in the way you aspire to live, work, and lead. You are putting into words what you want to give, share, and contribute to others.

Use this important time with yourself to reflect on the following questions that help you connect with your highest leadership aspirations:

- *Who are the leaders I admire?*
- *What behaviors and qualities am I drawn to in*

their leadership?

The answers you are looking for reflect your highest aspirations for yourself as a leader. When you think about the leaders you've admired and the leaders who've inspired you:

- *How would you describe the quality of their character and their connection with, and influence on people?*
- *What were their approaches, and how did they behave? What did you observe that you respected and admired?*

Your highest leadership aspirations are a result of reflections that help you define your higher purpose as a leader. They reflect what holds meaning for you in answering the question: *What kind of leader is it important for me to be and why?* The work of clarifying your highest aspirations will bring you in touch with what matters to you most, arriving at the heart of the matter for yourself. Your highest aspirations give you essential guidelines for your life and are the defining element of your *internal bearings*.

- *As a leader, what matters to me?*
- *What is my ideal for my leadership that is worth reaching for? What values and qualities distinguish my ideal?*

- *What legacy would I most like to leave? What would I like to be remembered for?*

Some useful things to consider: Every leader has to find his or her own way of putting their aspirations into words. When they do, their words hold great energy and meaning for them. As you find the words that best express your aspirations, you will have arrived at the *heart of the matter* for yourself; you will have captured what holds the greatest meaning for you at this important time in your life.

When you write down your aspirations, be conscious of allowing this to be a creative process, a chance to connect with the heart of what matters to you. Give yourself some room to expand your ideas without your internal criticizer taking over and being in charge. Take time to reflect—several days if necessary. Start with an initial draft of your ideas. At first you may find yourself listing activities. Take a break for a few minutes and then return to what you have written and ask yourself:

- *What do I aspire to that will lead me to these choices and actions?*

This leads to a deeper level of thought and intention.

Step 2: Balancing my *grit* and *gravitas*: Examining foibles and flaws through a constructive lens.

Below are descriptive examples of the imbalances that can characterize one's *grit* and *gravitas*. Use these lists to clarify current imbalances in your *grit* and *gravitas*. The examples we cite are meant to jog your thought process. Not every listed descriptive example will apply to you. See these imbalances through a *constructive* rather than a judgmental lens. Make notes for yourself as to how these factors may be getting in your way and preventing you from attaining your highest leadership aspirations.

We'll start below with the imbalances of *grit*.

Definition of *grit*: An uncompromising commitment to performance, excellence, and strategic focus. This refers to elements such as reliability, persistence, and collaboration, along with consistent follow-through:

- A drive to improve the organization's environment through the use of design frameworks that increase precision and effectiveness. Examples include placing the right people in the right roles, establishing the right structures and processes, and identifying the right standards.

- Boldness that conveys confidence.
- Analysis that allows for calculated risks.
- Confronting difficulties and challenges when they arise in order to take constructive action.
- Standing up for what it takes to be on track to meet goals and commitments: decisiveness, clarity, and accountability.

Too much *grit*

People with an imbalance of too much *grit* can come across as:

- ***Close-minded, dug in:*** Appearing inflexible, rigid, dug in, stubborn, lacking an inclination to consider the merits of other perspectives. Someone who is seen in this way tends to also lack an inclination for cooperation. He or she may come across as not valuing others for their input and information if they don't agree with their thinking. They may also tend to operate from an investment in their assumptions, thinking they are right, without verifying the validity of their assumptions.
- ***Dominating, controlling, "my way or the highway:"*** Behaving in a domineering, demanding, insistent manner; others experience this kind of person as inconsiderate and

controlling. This imbalance in someone's *grit* often comes across as a commanding influence, at times expressed through ultimatums, making their dissatisfaction apparent, and indicating others will either conform to his or her desires or else—it is clear that there will be consequences. This imbalance leads to behavior that is often experienced as demeaning and disrespectful.

- ***Micromanaging rather than empowering others:*** Someone who micromanages others exercises excessive control and involvement in details. Rather than empower others, they are inclined to either breathe down people's necks or "do it myself to get it done right." A consequence of this imbalance in someone's *grit* is the lack of talent development and the withholding of information and opportunity.

- ***Blaming and judgmental:*** Someone with this imbalance in their *grit* is often dominated by their internal negative criticizer. They judge and find fault with themselves and others in disempowering ways. Rather than choosing the power to address the matters at hand in constructive ways, their judgmental outlook and criticisms are used to find fault, be right, and be justified.

- ***Oppositional, confrontational and combative:*** Someone with these imbalances in their *grit* takes an interpersonal approach that is openly competitive and focused on winning at all costs. Sometimes they use below-the-belt tactics to diminish or discredit others in order to achieve advantage. These behaviors can be experienced as aggressive and disruptive, resulting in short-term and/or long-term consequences. These imbalances get in the way of progress. They create disunity and leave ill will, distrust, and resentment in their wake.

- ***Avoidance of authority:*** Someone with this imbalance in their *grit* has an aversion to expectations and demands from others in authority. They avoid being held accountable because they have difficulty with authority and have trouble aligning and working collaboratively with others; they resist what they experience as being told what to do. With their extreme need for independence and autonomy, they cannot recognize the value of collaborating and aligning with others.

Too little *grit* can look like:

- ***Ambivalent and conflicted, lacking the ability to select priorities and be decisive:*** Someone with this imbalance in their *grit* has trouble making decisions in a timely way. Their fear of making a wrong decision leaves them confused and ambivalent. The fear of failing causes overthinking and overanalyzing and gets in the way of choosing priorities and making strategic decisions.

- ***Lack of clarity when giving or receiving directions and setting expectations:*** Someone with this imbalance in their *grit,* on the one hand, doesn't set clear priorities or ensure that others have the information they need to execute plans and next steps. On the other hand, when receiving directions and the expectations involved, they don't always clarify because they don't want to feel or look stupid or be perceived as annoying by asking questions.

- ***Discomfort with power, one's own and other's:*** When someone has this imbalance in their *grit*, they feel uncomfortable with their own power and with the power others have. They may feel intimidated or lack confidence. Reluctant to stand up for themselves, they may be too eager to please and not want to make waves. Not wanting to impose on others, they bend over backwards; they take on too little or too much in tasks or projects, they don't push back in moments that matter, and they don't set boundaries. This discomfort leaves them feeling overwhelmed and burdened, which can lead to burnout.

- **Difficulty holding others to account:** Someone with this imbalance in their *grit* avoids the discomfort of confronting someone who isn't meeting expectations or coming through as agreed. They may avoid having difficult conversations because they don't want to seem demanding; they may confuse the importance of holding people accountable with being seen as overbearing. They often have a fear of conflict and an aversion to contentious dialogue with people who have difficulty being held accountable. Examples include people who act like the victim, people who become defensive and righteous and always have reasons for why things are the way they are, and mercurial people who refuse to be pinned down to what is, in fact, their responsibility.

- **Avoiding difficult conversations and emotionally charged situations:** Someone with this imbalance in their *grit* lacks skills for understanding emotions, reactions, and how to approach them constructively. Without these skills, he or she lacks the ability and confidence to access their emotions. Situations such as these trigger a threat rather than an opportunity. Without emotional intelligence skills, suppressed feelings can generate reactions expressed in unconstructive ways. The consequence often leads to misunderstandings, disunity, and blocked progress.

- ***Inconsistent behavior with a consequential effect of seeming or actually being unreliable:*** Someone with this imbalance in their *grit* lacks focus—they often lose the thread of where they were headed. They may have a pattern of showing up late for appointments and meetings, not holding up their end, not following through or keeping their word, which causes doubts as to their dependability and trustworthiness. They often find justifications for their behavior such as "being too busy." They can sound cavalier as if they lack concern and regard for others.

- ***Disorganized and lacking structures:*** Someone with this imbalance in their *grit* resists using structured and systematic approaches. Their imbalance can result in becoming disorganized and overwhelmed by keeping everything they have to do in their head. They resist using systems, for example, on their computer or journal to help them prioritize, complete tasks, and reach deadlines. Often their office can be messy and disorganized with files piled high on every surface. People with this imbalance in their *grit* have a pattern of creating chaos and causing confusion for themselves and others. They create obstacles that increase difficulty in getting work done.

Take a moment to identify any imbalances of *grit* you see in your leadership. For each imbalance you've identified:

- *Describe how this imbalance shows up in your leadership.*
- *How would this imbalance get in the way of your ability to lead from your highest aspirations?*

Definition of *gravitas*: A depth of professional knowledge and competence that contributes to excellence in performance. This refers to elements such as:

- Expertise, competence, and capability
- Credibility
- Depth, breadth of knowledge, and experience
- Role, title, and status

Too much *gravitas* can look like:

- ***Hubris, expressing opinions with an air of superiority:*** Because of their considerable experience and expertise, someone with this imbalance in their *gravitas* often dominates conversations in what feels condescending to others. Without realizing it, they speak with a careless lack of humility. Their arrogance causes them to correct and criticize others and come across with an air of superiority. Someone with this imbalance in their *gravitas* is overly concerned with their own desires, needs, or interests to the exclusion of others. This gets in the way of collaborating, cooperating, or functioning as a constructive member of a team.

- ***Thinking one's opinion is the only one that matters:*** Someone with this imbalance in their *gravitas* often goes on and on seeming pedantic, speaking only on "send" and not listening to "receive." Someone with this imbalance talks over others and interrupts; they can exhibit a pattern of selective listening. They seem to ignore, minimize, or invalidate the importance of what others have to say. This prevents them from recognizing the value inherent in listening to the perspectives, opinions, and inputs that others have to contribute. Another consequence is that people can be left frustrated, potentially resentful, and become disengaged.

- ***Acting in an obstructive and controlling manner:*** Someone with this imbalance in their *gravitas* uses controlling behavior, which interferes with and obstructs the flow of progress. They use justifications such as "They don't know what they're doing" or "I'm just being a devil's advocate." Their obstructive and controlling behavior makes it more difficult to accomplish what needs to be done.

- ***Gravitas that others perceive as unapproachable and intimidating***: While it's not the person or expert's intent, sometimes someone with *gravitas* in their field or profession can be perceived as intimidating and unapproachable because of their considerable knowledge or ability when, in fact, they may be shy and introverted. Someone with this imbalance in their *gravitas* may lack the skills that would allow them to be more connected and at ease in collaborating with their teammates and colleagues. Unlike someone who lauds their knowledge over people, these are people who, because of their shyness and introversion, wind up isolated and excluded.

- ***Keeping others at a disadvantage:*** Using one's *gravitas* to assert and protect one's own status as a source of value above others while directly or indirectly diminishing what others bring to the table. Someone with this imbalance in their *gravitas* defaults to competitive power plays; for instance, they often take credit for work that others have contributed to or originated. Some of the ways they keep others at a disadvantage are by withholding time, attention, cooperation, inclusion, resources, recognition, and/or support. The consequences of these behaviors are the loss of collaboration—blended *gravitas*—and the potential for synergistic problem solving, breakthrough thinking, and innovative progress.

Too little *gravitas* can look like:

- **Unclaimed *gravitas*, coming across to others as lacking in strength, stature, and significance:** Unlike humility, which downplays *recognized* abilities, unclaimed *gravitas* reflects an inability or a reticence to adequately recognize one's depth of knowledge and experience. Someone with this imbalance in their *gravitas* robs themselves of the quiet confidence, credibility, and stature that comes from authentically recognizing one's *gravitas*. Some of the repercussions can take the form of being discounted, passed over, disregarded, or excluded.

- **An absence of internal permission to own one's power and influence:** Someone with this imbalance in their *gravitas* has a lack of confidence in their knowledge and experience, which results in an imbalance in their *grit*—the reluctance to push back, take a stand, or contribute an idea, a perspective, or an observation that could be of value to the matters at hand. This imbalance in one's *gravitas* reflects an absence of internal permission to express one's power and influence. It is all too easy for someone with this imbalance to minimize their accomplishments, their growth, and their development. Their self-confidence suffers as a result. Retreating from important and meaningful opportunities, their lack of confidence impedes or blocks their progress and gets in the way of achieving their considerable potential. As a result, they take on too little; they play too small.

- **Overcompensating, trying too hard to be seen as credible:** Someone with this imbalance in their *gravitas* often tries to prove their value and worthiness. In their efforts to be perceived as capable and credible, they often take on more than they can handle. They also try too hard to be liked and accepted. Someone with this imbalance in their *gravitas* may accept responsibilities without understanding how to build the appropriate platforms and garner the necessary advocacy, resources, and support they need to succeed. To mask their insecurities, they often present a patina of confidence; they overcompensate for a lack of authentic confidence in themselves, which makes them appear inauthentic to others.

- **Lacking strategic thinking skills or lacking vision:** Someone with this imbalance in their *gravitas* loses their grasp of the big picture. Their analytic brilliance often has them get caught up in the details. Having zoomed in to analyze the details, they find themselves unable to zoom back out again to see the connections and possibilities that could lead to breakthroughs, innovation, and growth.

Take a moment to identify any imbalances of *gravitas* you see in your leadership. For each imbalance you've identified:

- *Describe how this imbalance shows up in your leadership.*
- *How would this imbalance get in the way of your ability to lead from your highest aspirations?*

For the purposes of your development—no judging allowed—list the top three imbalances that stood out for you (it's okay if you only have one or two). You will have a chance to see how you can transform them as we consider the elements of *grace* in the next step below.

Definition of *grace*: To begin with, *grace* rests on the two pillars of *reaction management* and *relationship intelligence*. Grace unleashes *constructive power* in a leader's presence. It elevates the quality and effectiveness of a leader's interactions and influence in empowering people, performance, and outcomes.

***Grace* is a combination of:**

- A depth of knowledge and ability to transform negative human emotions and dynamics into constructive dialogue and outcomes.
- An understanding of the social brain and the ability of a leader to bring people together through considerate, thoughtful means that

serve the needs of those they lead.

Step 3: Applying the skills of Reaction Management and Relationship Intelligence to imbalances in my *grit* and *gravitas*.

Take a few moments to reflect on the specific skills involved in the two pillars of *grace*: *reaction management* and *relationship intelligence*. Make some notes as you consider each skill below that applies to the two or three imbalances you identified.

Reaction management

(See Chapter 3.)

Reaction management provides a leader with knowledge that impacts his or her ability to move more quickly beyond the negative states of reactions. A leader is then able to access the brain's remarkable capacity to see and take constructive approaches—ones that resolve and remove barriers to achieving desired results.

Below are some of the critical *reaction management* skills leaders have integrated and used to transform their leadership and the impact of their presence. These elements serve as a map you can follow and apply:

- Train yourself to recognize when you are in the *reactive zone*.
- Press the pause button to help you stay out of the *reactive zone*. Build the habit of *pausing* when an emotional reaction takes hold. Notice what is going on inside of you, mentally and physically. Start to notice what emotions and thoughts you are experiencing.
- Train yourself to move out of "fight or flight" mode to regain access to your higher order thinking to 1) see and take effective measures to resolve what triggered the reaction you are having, and 2) choose a constructive, rather than reactive response.
    - Identify where you are feeling tension (for example, tightening in the neck, back, gritting teeth). Breathe into the tension.
    - Name the emotion to decrease its intensity.
    - Ask yourself questions that increase your awareness such as: *Why do I feel threatened? What happened in this situation that isn't sitting right with me? What other emotions am I feeling? Are expectations, values, or boundaries involved?*
    - Clarify for yourself what would be the

most constructive outcome in this situation? Determine a possible resolution for the situation and all involved. *How might I/we resolve this issue and go on in a better way?*
- o Elevate negative emotional states: Use your *constructive power* to neutralize negativity and keep reactive states from escalating. Ask a question such as: *What are your thoughts about what is happening?* Then listen, listen, listen! Seek to understand. Diffuse negativity by paraphrasing, letting others know you understand their feelings and their concerns.
- o When you use your constructive power, others will recognize this. It will be evident in your approaches, behaviors, connection with others, and your demeanor.

Relationship intelligence

(See Chapters 4, 5, and 6.)

Relationship intelligence provides a leader with knowledge of emotions, how and why they affect people and their performance, and the skills involved in elevating emotional states from negative to neutral to positive. With its roots in brain science and emotional intelligence, relationship intelligence provides critical knowledge for bringing out the best in people and empowering them when it matters most.

Below are some of the critical *relationship intelligence* skills leaders have integrated and used to transform their leadership and the impact of their presence. The elements below can serve as a map you can follow and apply:

- **Establish psychological safety.** When psychological safety is provided, you create the conditions for trust. When issues and challenges arise, psychological safety allows the men and women you lead to have difficult conversations in productive ways. This helps them generate constructive outcomes.

- **Establish ground rules.** As part of establishing psychological safety, set ground rules. For example, instead of looking for who or what is to blame, let's look at what occurred in the context of having a *conversation for resolution, gaining understanding, identifying next steps, and generating progress.*

- **Use generous listening.** A critical part of elevating emotional states and of empowering and bringing out the best in others.

  - Listen to understand rather than to judge.
  - Listen to learn and to gain insight to understand how best to proceed.
  - Paraphrase to reflect what you have heard someone say.
  - Ask if you are missing anything in what you've paraphrased.
  - Look back over your notes and review the imbalances you've identified. Use the following questions to clarify the *reaction management* and *relationship intelligence* skills that will help you achieve your highest aspirations as a leader.

For each imbalance in *grit* and *gravitas* you have chosen, consider the following questions, writing down your answers:

- Taking one imbalance at a time: *How will addressing this imbalance make a difference in achieving my aspirations and my leadership?* For example, one leader said they would "stop cutting people off when they are speaking and work on being a better listener."

- *If I were a better leader three months from now than I am today, what would be different in the way I lead?* For example, one leader recognized that by developing others he would be able to delegate, rather than do it all himself. He saw how this would allow him to take on greater levels of responsibility and oversight.
- *What would I do differently in my important relationships?* Below are some areas to consider:
  - *What changes could I make in how I:*

Listen

_____

Communicate

_____

Focus my attention

_____

Manage my reactions and emotions

_____

Show my respect and appreciation

_____

Meet challenges and face conflict

_____

o *What small steps will get me started?*

As you continue to clarify and lead from your *internal bearings,* you will find yourself leading in a very different way. Your approaches, behaviors, the quality of your connection with people, and your demeanor will reflect your *highest leadership aspirations*. As you build strength in developing your *reaction management* and *relationship intelligence skills*, you will harness the *constructive power of grace*. By integrating the skills and qualities of *grace* into your *grit* and your *gravitas*, you will hold the keys to transforming your leadership, your impact, and your presence.

Resources

Ariel Fox, Erica, *Winning From Within: A Breakthrough Method for Leading, Living, and Lasting Change*, 2013, NYC, NY, Harper Business.

Barsade, Sigal, "Employee emotions aren't noise—they're data: Emotions provide insight into what motivates people and how to improve performance," *MIT Sloan Management Review*, November 2019, p. 138. https://sloanreview.mit.edu/article/employee-emotions-arent-noise-theyre-data/#article-authors

Bates, Suzanne, and Macaux, William, *All the Leader You Can Be: The Science of Achieving Extraordinary Executive Presence*, 2016, NYC, NY, McGraw-Hill Education.

Beeson, John, *The Unwritten Rules: The Six Skills You Need to Get Promoted to the Executive Level*, 2010, San Francisco, CA, Jossey-Bass.

Cain, Susan, *Quiet: The Power of Introverts in a World That Can't Stop Talking*, 2013, New York City, NY, Crown Publishing Group.

Cooper Hakim, Amy, and Sullivan, Muriel, *Working With Difficult People: Handling the Ten Types of Problem People Without Losing Your Mind*, 1990, NYC, New York, Penguin Random House LLC.

Covey, Stephen M. R., with Merrill, Rebecca R., *The Speed of Trust: The One Thing That Changes Everything*, 2006, Florence, MA, Free Press.

Coyle, Daniel, *The Culture Code: The Secret of Highly Successful Groups*, 2018, NYC, NY, Bantam Books.

Cuddy, Amy, *Presence: Bringing Your Boldest Self to Your Biggest Challenges*, 2015, NYC, NY, Little, Brown and Company.

Dagley, Dr. Gavin R. "Executive Presence: Influence Beyond Authority," https://workingwithourselves.files.wordpress.com/2009/03/executive-presence-report-g-dagley-2013.pdf

Duhigg, Charles, *The Power of Habit: Why We Do What We Do in Life and Business*, 2014, NYC, NY, Penguin Random House Company.

Edmondson, Amy C., *The Fearless Organization: Creating Psychological Safety in the Workplace for*

Learning, Innovation, and Growth, 2019, Hoboken, NJ, John Wiley & Sons, Inc.

Frankl, Victor E., *Man's Search for Meaning: The Classic Tribute to Hope From the Holocaust*, 2001, UK, Rider Books.

George, Bill, *Authentic Leadership: Rediscovering the Secrets to Creating Lasting Value*, 2003, San Francisco, CA, Jossey-Bass.

George, Bill, *True North: Discover Your Authentic Leadership*, 2007, San Francisco, CA, Jossey-Bass.

George, Bill, *Seven Lessons for Leading in Crisis*, 2009, San Francisco, CA, Jossey-Bass.

Goldsmith, Marshall, with Reiter, Mark, *What Got You Here, Won't Get You There: How Successful People Become Even More Successful*, 2007, NYC, NY, Hyperion.

Goldsmith, Marshall, *Succession: Are You Ready?*, 2009, Cambridge, MA, Harvard Business Press.

Goldsmith, Marshall, and Reiter, Mark, *Triggers: Creating Behavior That Lasts—Becoming the Person You Want to Be*, 2015, NYC, NY, Crown Publishing Group.

Grant, Adam M., *Give and Take: Why Helping Others Drives Our Success*, 2013, NYC, NY, Penguin Random House LLC.

Hedges, Kristi, *The Power of Presence: Unlock Your Potential to Influence and Engage Others*, 2011, NYC, NY, AMA.

Helgeson, Sally, and Goldsmith, Marshall, *How Women Rise—Being Fully Present*, 2018, NYC, NY, Hachette.

Hewlett, Sylvia Ann, *Executive Presence: The Missing Link Between Merit and Success*, 2014, NYC, NY, Harper Business.

Huffington, Arianna, *The Fourth Instinct: The Call of the Soul*, 1994, NYC, NY, Simon & Schuster.

Kahneman, Daniel, *Thinking, Fast and Slow*, 2011, NYC, NY, Farrar, Straus & Giroux.

Kaplan, Robert E., and Kaiser, Robert B., *Fear Your Strengths*, 2013, San Francisco, CA, Berrett-Koehler Publishers.

Kouzes, James M., and Posner, Barry Z., *Credibility: How Leaders Gain and Lose It, Why People Demand It*, 2011, San Francisco, CA, Jossey-Bass.

Kouzes, James M., and Posner, Barry Z., *The Leadership Challenge: How to Make Extraordinary*

Things Happen in Organizations, 2017, Hoboken, NJ, John Wiley & Sons, Inc.

Lieberman, Dr. Matthew D., *Social: Why Our Brains Are Wired to Connect*, 2013, NYC, NY, Crown Publishers.

McKay, Sarah, *The Women's Brain Book: The Neuroscience of Health, Hormones and Happiness*, 2018, Australia, Hachette Australia.

Rock, David, "SCARF: A brain-based model for collaborating with and influencing others," *NeuroLeadership Journal*, Issue 1, 2008.

Rock, David, "Managing with the Brain in Mind," *Strategy+Business*, Issue 56, August 27, 2009.

Talk: "What makes a good life? Lessons from the longest study on happiness" by Robert Waldinger, https://www.youtube.com/watch?v=8KkKuTCFvzI

Additional article: "Harvard's longest study of adult life reveals how you can be happier and more successful" https://www.cnbc.com/2018/03/20 /this-harvard-study-reveals-how-you-can-be-happier-and-more-successful.html